Telecommuting
The Organizational and Behavioral Effects of Working at Home

Research for Business Decisions, No. 75

Richard N. Farmer, Series Editor

Professor of International Business
Indiana University

Other Titles in This Series

Telecommuting
The Organizational and Behavioral Effects of Working at Home

by
Reagan Mays Ramsower

UMI RESEARCH PRESS
Ann Arbor, Michigan

Produced and distributed by
UMI Research Press
an imprint of
University Microfilms International
A Xerox Information Resources Company
Ann Arbor, Michigan 48106

Library of Congress Cataloging in Publication Data

Ramsower, Reagan Mays, 1952-
   Telecommuting: the organizational and behavioral
effects of working at home.

   (Research for business decisions ; no. 75)
   Revision of thesis (Ph.D.)—University of Minnesota, 1983.
   Bibliography: p.
   Includes index.
   1. Telecommuting—United States.   I. Title.
II. Series.
HD2336.U5R36   1985   658.3'12   84-28095
ISBN 0-8357-1628-7 (alk. paper)

For Jason, Who Shared His Father's Time and Attention

Contents

List of Figures

List of Tables

1

The Electronic Cottage

Hidden inside our advance to a new production system is a potential for social change so breathtaking in scope that few among us have been willing to face its meaning. For we are about to revolutionize our homes as well.[1]

Alvin Toffler was predicting the beginning of a new age with a production system which would create a new work site — the "Electronic Cottage." This would be the third great era of economic production to occur in the history of man. Each of the previous two epochs largely obliterated earlier cultures or civilizations and replaced them with completely new ways of life.

The Agricultural Revolution was the First Wave of production change. Over a period of several thousand years, man went from a herding and roaming lifestyle to one based on collective farming communities. In only three hundred years, the Second Wave of change, the Industrial Revolution, brought man from the lifestyle of farming into one characterized by industrial cities and central business districts. According to Toffler, the Third Wave will require only a few decades to implant its new production system and transport man from the urban office back to the pre-industrial work place — the home. It will be characterized as highly technical but anti-industrial, utilizing technology to provide more individual freedom of expression and work.

Watching masses of peasants scything a field three hundred years ago, only a madman would have dreamed that the time would have come when the fields would be depopulated, when people would crowd into urban factories to earn their daily bread. And only a madman would have been right. Today it takes an act of courage to suggest that our biggest factories and office towers may, within our lifetimes, stand half empty, reduced to use as ghostly warehouses or converted into living space. Yet this is precisely what the new mode of production makes possible: a return to cottage industry on a new, higher, electronic basis, and with it a new emphasis on the home as the center of society.[2]

What developments in the Third Wave's "Electronic Cottage" have occurred since Toffler's predictive madness in 1980? Even as Toffler wrote, the emergence of the Third Wave's production system was becoming visible. Western countries were being increasingly characterized as "information societies"[3] in which a majority of the work force was engaged in the storage, transfer, or manipulation of information. The growth of "information industries" such as banking, insurance, finance, accounting, government, and education far surpassed that of the manufacturing and raw material producers that were characteristic of the Second Wave.[4] Information workers were often seen "huddled around computers" because of their dependency upon information and the related information technology.[5]

More recent advances and implementations in telecommunications are now serving to free these workers from the need to be in close proximity to the computer. Technological advancements have begun to dramatically alter the organizational work structure and the process of doing business. The "destructive restructuring" of business has begun.[6] Information can be transported more cheaply than people, and industries are beginning to recognize the possibilities of these new economies. "It is our shared philosophy that it is cheaper to move information than people."[7]

The 1975 census showed 3.2 percent of the work force was employed at home. Of these, one-third were farmers and the remainder were in business for themselves.[8]

Indeed, an unmeasured but appreciable amount of work is already being done at home by such people as salesmen and saleswomen who work by phone or visit, and only occasionally touch base at the office; by architects and designers; by a burgeoning pool of specialized consultants in many industries; by large numbers of human-service workers like therapists or psychologists; by music teachers and language instructors, by art dealers, investment counselors, insurance agents, lawyers, and academic researchers; and by many other categories of white-collar, technical, and professional people.[9]

Current interest in working at home goes far beyond this group of home workers. Telecommuting is the use of computer and telecommunications technologies which permits organizational employees to substitute telecommunications for transportation thereby permitting some or all of a job to be performed at a remote work site. As such, telecommuting could enormously increase the number of people in the information industries who would work at home.

The popular literature contains some accounts of operational experiments with telecommuting. For example, recent *Business Week* (January 26, 1981) and *New York Times* (March 12, 1981) articles cite a variety of business and industry experiments with telecommuting. No one claims however, that telecommuting is occurring on a large scale, but observers such as Harvey Poppel of Booz, Allen and Hamilton and Jack Nilles at the University of Southern California have estimated that within ten years telecommuting could become widespread, approaching fifteen to twenty percent of the workforce.[10] However, these estimates are based upon very limited information concerning the types of jobs and workers which would be suitable for telecommuting.

The major categories of jobs and workers thought to be most suitable to telecommuting are the managerial, professional, and clerical levels involving, for example, various kinds of managers, information analysts, computer professionals, and information or word processing clerks. "Indeed, several studies have concluded that a large number of managerial, clerical, and professional functions could be performed by using various modes of telecommunications, provided that certain additional criteria were met."[11]

Some banks and other organizations have placed word processing machines in the homes of secretaries. By combining the power of the microcomputer with telecommunication capabilities, the "electronic briefcase" could allow many executives to work from their homes.

Given the right telecommunications almost any white-collar work could be done at home. Secretaries can type there or answer telephones. Typing pools can be distributed. Accountants can work with terminals at home. In writing a report, a group of authors can type the text directly into their respective home terminals. The report resides in the memory of a distant machine. They can then modify it, edit it, restructure it, snip bits out, correct each other's work, add to each other's ideas, and instruct the terminal to type clean copies when they are ready. Magazine editing will be done with such aids in the future.[12]

These estimates concerning the future of telecommuting and the jobs which can be performed at home do not account for one of the critical success factors of telecommuting, namely, "will organizations and people find telecommuting desirable?" The organizational and behavioral effects of telecommuting are largely or completely unknown. It would seem that it has been implicitly assumed that a telecommuter's job would be more enriched. However, common sense would seem to indicate just the opposite. The days when it was believed that the primary motivation to work was monetary are past. People work because of social and achievement needs, and telecommuting may in fact be very detrimental to satisfying such needs through work. Additionally, people work in central offices for reasons besides the simple sharing of information. The central work site often provides synergism, *esprit de corps*, and a place where new employees are trained. People could be monitored electronically in their homes, but supervisors may not adopt this style of management willingly, and employees may reel against the "big brother" methods of electronic monitoring.

This study is a preliminary step towards an understanding of the organizational and behavioral consequences of telecommuting. As such, it will provide valuable information concerning the extent to which telecommuting should be considered as a work alternative for various jobs and individuals.

2

Pros and Cons of Telecommuting

Reasons for Telecommuting

While the idea of using computer and telecommunications technology to allow a large proportion of the work force to work at home is relatively new, several social and technical reasons for doing so have been proposed. These reasons are in response to several influences which are quite distinct from previous motivations to utilize home workers.

> The trend to remote work today represents a significant break from past examples because of two major influences in organizations and society. These two influences are highly interrelated: One is the changing nature of work itself, and the second is the telecommunications revolution.[1]

Social Reasons

The social factors which have changed the nature of work and increased interest in telecommuting are:

1. A greater value being placed upon the quality of working life.
2. The increased commuting distances required in today's cities.
3. A shift in attitudes concerning the family unit.

The first social reason for telecommuting is based upon the untested assumption that telecommuting will improve the quality of work life.

> One option for improving quality of work life is providing alternative work arrangements both in space and time. The total effect of providing a more satisfactory work environment (for the individual) and greater flexibility in work hours, in addition to reducing the stress of commuting, should result in greater motivation and job satisfaction and reduced turnover for the organization.[2]

The importance of a high quality working life in career decisions is especially true for people with specialized skills who are increasing in numbers as the information society develops. For example, today's computer professionals report that salary is of much less value after they are hired than the quality of working life.[3] The opportunity to utilize flexible work options is having an increasing appeal for these workers. They value the ability to work self-determined hours, at a self-determined pace, in a self-determined casual wardrobe.[4]

The second social reason for telecommuting is found in the development of large central business districts which have increased the commuting distances of workers. As the workday becomes shorter, the longer their commuting time becomes relative to it. Employees may refuse to invest the same commuting time if the hours spent on the job are cut. "The higher the ratio of commuting time to working time, the more irrational, frustrating, and absurd the process of shuttling back and forth."[5] Employers have to increase the premium paid to workers in these big, centralized work locations, relative to those willing to take less pay for less travel time, inconvenience, and cost. One Houston oil company pays $75.00 a month in travel fees to its commuting workers.

A third social reason for telecommuting concerns the changes in attitudes toward the "family unit." The emergence of dual career families is forcing both companies and couples to look for compromise situations in the event of transfers. Additionally, for some groups, such as the elderly, severely handicapped, and single parents with young children, telecommuting may also provide an opportunity to utilize valuable skills that could not be used otherwise.[6]

Technical Reasons

Besides the social reasons for telecommuting, advances in information and communications technologies are also behind the increased interest in working at home. These advances provide the capability of substituting various modes of telecommuting technologies such as remote computer terminals, word processing stations, teleconferencing, and/or telecommunications-based neighborhood work centers for intracity travel. The shift from Toffler's Second Wave manufacturing to the new, more advanced "information society" of the Third Wave has reduced the number of workers who actually have to manipulate physical goods. "This means that even in the manufacturing sector, an increasing amount of work is being done that — given the right configuration of telecommunications and other equipment — could be accomplished anywhere, including one's own living room."[7]

Advanced technological capabilities, most of which are already in existence, although some are not yet economically practical, are serving as the catalyst to introduce telecommuting. There are many instances in which "organizations have remolded themselves, not in direct response to great ideas, but in response to the development of intervening technology that stimulates implementation of those ideas."[8]

The most important technological developments which are stimulating this interest in telecommuting are:

a) Low-cost communications available to everyone that are independent of distance.[9]
b) Low-cost computer power, especially the inexpensive microcomputer, which allows electronic intelligence to be placed in the home.[10]
c) Electronic communications services which permit personal communication as opposed to broadcast communications. The services particularly useful for telecommuting are electronic mail and teleconferencing.[11]

In the following discussion, a best case scenario is presented to illustrate some of the benefits of telecommuting which may occur if both the social and technical rationales prove valid.

The Best Case Scenario

An employee is assigned to begin working at home. While the spatial-physical distance is increased by this move, the use of the telephone, computer conferencing and electronic mail moderates the effects. Communication, both socially and work-related, remains at approximately the same level as before the move. Frequent phone and computer contact with the supervisor is maintained. The supervisor feels that the monitoring of the telecommuter's performance is as good, or better, than before. Use of telecommunications makes it quick and easy to send and receive work to and from the telecommuter.

The phone and computer terminal are capable of handling up to ninety percent of the telecommuter's conversations. When interactive communication is unnecessary, the telecommuter uses electronic mail to communicate asynchronously with co-workers, supervisors, and subordinates. All parties regularly read and respond to their electronic mail. The computer terminal and equipment are appropriate for the job and easily rival the equipment used in the office.

The telecommuter and supervisor find that the entire spectrum of job tasks of the telecommuter can be performed at home. Access to procedures and documentation used to perform the job tasks are on-line to the home computer or terminal. Help in the performance of the job can quickly be obtained using the terminal and/or telecommunications system.

The organizational behavior of the employee is improved dramatically. The trust and confidence bestowed upon the telecommuter by the organization is not betrayed. Using the technology to "stay in touch," the telecommuter retains a high identification with the work group and a strong feeling of being a part of the supervisor's team. The telecommuter enjoys the additional time which results from not commuting to work, the freedom of choosing work hours, the ability to take care of family responsibilities, and the casual atmosphere of the home. Attitude was initially positive towards working at home; it is now extremely positive. Job satisfaction has increased, and work related stress has decreased. As a result, performance is steadily improving, and the employee cannot visualize the day in which it would be desirable to work in the office again. The employee, supervisor, and co-workers have seen the emergence of Toffler's Third Wave.

In summary, the reasons for the current interest in telecommuting can be classified as both social and technical. The social reasons include the possibility that telecommuting will improve the quality of working life, that telecommuting will reduce the problem of commuting in today's cities, and that telecommuting coincides with a changing attitude concerning the "family unit." These social beliefs about telecommuting, coupled with the technical feasibility of allowing many workers to work at home, comprise the the current reasons for telecommuting.

Reasons against Telecommuting

> One should not underestimate the difficulties entailed in transferring work from its Second Wave locations in factory and office to its Third Wave location in the home. Problems of motivation and management, of corporate and social reorganization will make the shift both prolonged and, perhaps, painful. [12]

There are several reasons for not introducing telecommuting into an organization. These reasons are concerned with the cost of implementing the technical configuration, the loss of face-to-face communication and social contact associated with working at home, and the remote management of workers.

Economic Costs

A major reason against introducing telecommuting concerns the economic cost of placing the required computer and telecommunications equipment in the home of the telecommuter. While the technology to allow many workers to work from their homes is largely available, it is often too expensive to justify the social or productivity benefits which might be derived from telecommuting. Even though organizations and researchers are beginning to realize the importance of introducing electronic capital such as terminals and micro-computers into the productions systems of white-collar jobs, it will be many years before all employees in these jobs have their own "electronic briefcases."

Unless telecommuting can be shown to increase a worker's performance by an amount which offsets the economic investment in the electronic capital needed to work at home, organizations will not adopt telecommuting.

Loss of Communication and Social Contact

Another reason against the introduction of telecommuting concerns the loss of face-to-face communication imposed by telecommuting. Some of the jobs of information workers, especially those involving creative deal-making where the decisions are nonroutine, require a high level of face-to-face contact. The bandwidths of the various telecommunications mediums are not wide enough to handle the communication of body language, subtle meanings, and implied gestures. For these workers, this level of communication is paramount to the acceptable performance of their jobs, and it would appear that telecommuting would be unacceptable.

Telecommuting will also produce a loss in the social contact associated with today's office. It may be foolish to assume that the general body of information workers would be willing to give up this social contact in favor of the isolation of their homes. However, some individuals may not mind the loss either because of low social needs or because telecommuting is the only way in which they can work given their personal situation (i.e. individuals that are handicapped, have young children in the home, or are located at great distance from their work). While a few individuals actually prefer to work alone, most workers involved in telecommuting do mind the loss of social interaction. They "would prefer their old arrangement or some new arrangement permitting closer interaction with fellow workers; some workers have returned to office work."[13]

Remote Management of Workers

Finally, a major reason against organizations becoming involved with telecommuting relates to the management and supervision of remote workers. When work can be parceled out on a project basis with a fixed cost or fee attached, this problem is largely eliminated. However, if work cannot be so parceled out (because of the nature of the work or because employees resist the remuneration agreement), supervision and management of a remote worker is more difficult than in the office.[14] If accurate measures of the worker's performance cannot be obtained this problem is even further compounded.

The Worst Case Scenario

A worst case scenario is presented based upon the reasons against telecommuting. This scenario demonstrates that telecommuting can be very detrimental to both the organization and the telecommuting employee.

An employee is assigned to begin working from home. This move creates a considerable increase in the spatial-physical distance between the employee and the organization. To compensate, the organization installs an expensive terminal and printer in the employee's home after considerable trouble and expense. However, even with this equipment, social and job related communications decrease substantially. As a result of this remoteness, the employee's visibility within the company drops to a very low level. Co-workers become strangers. Contact with the employee's supervisor and subordinates also drops dramatically. Performance monitoring and measurement becomes virtually nonexistent, and the supervisor experiencing the "out of sight, out of mind" phenomenon loses respect for the employee and no longer considers the employee for advancement within the company. Work ceases to flow properly to and from the remote worker so that getting job assignments and completing tasks on a timely basis becomes very difficult.

The employee tries to "keep in touch" by using the phone and computer terminal. The telecommuter finds that phone discussions are too limited and narrow and that people resent being bothered by the phone. Computer communications do not work either, since people do not read their electronic mail, and the telecommunication system is largely useless. The computer terminal and equipment is inadequate for the telecommuter's job. Output is too slow, and hardcopy too difficult to obtain for the effective performance of the telecommuter's job.

As a result of these problems the telecommuter is limited to only a few highly independent tasks with short time frames. This greatly reduces the value of the employee to the organization. The complexity of performing the job tasks gradually increases due to a lack of contact and access to individuals, procedures, and documentation which are needed to correctly perform the job.

The organizational behavior of the employee begins to suffer severely. Individual commitment and interest in the organization and job slowly disappear. The remote worker begins to lose identification with the work group and no longer feels a part of the supervisor's team. While the employee's initial attitude towards working at home was positive, it now becomes largely negative. Rather than being more satisfied with the work, a feeling of disfranchisement is experienced. Performance drops dramatically as the employee develops less motivation to work. The employee, supervisor, and co-workers have seen the folly of working at home.

3

Corporate Experiences

During 1981 and 1982, interest in telecommuting programs increased dramatically. By the middle of 1982, one popular magazine estimated that as many as six hundred workers in thirty-five organizations were telecommuting."[1] These organizations reported that they introduced telecommuting to:

- Enrich the jobs of their workers.
- Attract employees from the home-bound labor pool.
- Reduce office space overhead and commuting costs.

A brief review of some of these telecommuting programs is presented in this chapter. It should be noted that the results and conclusions stated in the following discussion are based upon very limited and often subjective information taken from the popular literature. The author could not find a single case in which an empirical organizational experiment of telecommuting was undertaken and publicly reported. Therefore, this discussion should be viewed as one that espouses the currently held beliefs about telecommuting which are largely without substantiation.

Telecommuting to Enrich the Employee's Job

Many of the organizations which introduced telecommuting based their rationale upon the assumption that telecommuting would enrich the jobs of the telecommuters. This assumption led many organizations to conclude that by allowing their workers to telecommute they will be able to attract and retain valuable employees in certain key skilled areas.

Many computer companies are in the forefront of the trend to introduce telecommuting. Digital Equipment, Data General, and Control Data all provide work-at-home programs. A spokesman for Digital Equipment indicated that, "As prices of computer hardware come down, it becomes ever more practical to install work equipment at home when desired." At Data General, the feeling was expressed that allowing people to work at home is a natural work site evolution as computer technology develops.[2]

Control Data Corporation has about one hundred employees working at home or at satellite offices in an energy-saving, production-raising experiment called the "Alternative Work Site Program." Analysts, computer programmers, managers, education-course writers, and clerical workers are employed in this program. Initial reports[3] indicate that telecommuting:

- Reduces monthly auto driving
- Increases productivity
- Reduces turnover
- Reduces the need to relocate workers

These reported outcomes support the contention that telecommuting can enrich the jobs of telecommuters.

Several other organizations have also reported that telecommuting has increased their organization's ability to attract and retain valuable employees.[4] A supplier of software products, Interactive Systems Corporation, has several employees working at home or in satellite offices. They report several incidents in which telecommuting allowed them to retain or attract valuable employees by increasing or preserving an employee's quality of working life. For instance, they reported that one employee who worked at headquarters decided to move to another city, four hundred miles away. He was a senior company researcher who wanted to continue to work for them; therefore, the company decided that it was possible to let him work out of his new home using one of the company's microcomputers. In three other cases, the company was able to hire computer scientists to work on specific research projects even though the three professionals preferred not to work at an existing company site, but from their homes — in Massachusetts, Texas, and Colorado.[5]

Telecommuting is also important to another company, Country Programmers International, which uses at-home professional programmers who prefer the rural rather than the urban lifestyle. The founder of Country Programmers started the company after moving to rural Vermont to escape the "urban rat race," and found "a lot of other computer people . . . who'd given up good salaries in order to escape."[6]

These reports indicate that while telecommuting did not increase the intrinsic task characteristics of these jobs, it did appear to increase the extrinsic task characteristics associated with the working environment. It was claimed that this outcome resulted in the ability to retain and/or attract employees.

Telecommuting to Employ the Home-bound

A shortage of workers in some areas led several organizations to introduce telecommuting in an effort to tap into the home-bound labor force. The home-bound labor force is comprised of individuals who, for reasons such as physical handicaps or having responsibility for primary child care, are unable to work in locations other than their homes. Several organizations report that telecommuting allowed them to employ home-bound individuals often at reduced or contract wages. The competitive advantage realized by utilizing the home-bound labor force was often sufficient enough to make these organizations profitable.

F International is a computer related company which is based upon telecommuting. The company's workforce consists of contract telecommuters who work at home on either a part-time or full-time basis.[7] Sixty percent of their telecommuters are women who want to work at home because they have child-care responsibilities.[8]

Other organizations have utilized telecommuting to employ home-bound individuals for word processing or data entry jobs. Continental Illinois National Bank & Trust in Chicago has hired a group of word processors to work at home.[9] These individuals receive their dictation over the phone lines, type the material using a home word processing system, then send the typed material back to the office via telecommunications where it is printed and distributed. Blue Cross and Blue Shield in South Carolina employs several "cottage keyers" who enter seventy percent of the company's claims from home terminals. Blue Cross and Blue Shield report that the telecommuters have shorter cycle times for the processing of claims and lower error rates. Savings on turnover and absenteeism have also been reported.[10]

At least one organization has explored at-home work for handicapped individuals. Lift Incorporated, a nonprofit organization, has trained about thirty handicapped individuals to program computers from terminals in their homes.[11]

Telecommuting to Reduce Office and Commuting Costs

The costs of real estate and energy for many organizations has increased to a point where some companies see telecommuting as justified because it reduces office overhead and employee commuting costs. Expanding work facilities in metropolitan areas can be very expensive. "Space in many business centers is at a premium, not only in price but in availability. Heat, air conditioning, lighting, maintenance, parking, and security are higher priced items in large urban facilities."[12] It has been suggested that telecommuting offers a work option which could relieve the company of the necessity to furnish office space and the normal conveniences associated with that space. "Their capital investment requirements would shrink and insurance rates would drop drastically."[13] Additionally, most companies either directly or indirectly subsidize commuting. For example, in New York City, employees work only a thirty-five-hour week, but are paid for forty. "Companies in metropolitan areas pay higher salaries, basically to subsidize commuting costs."[14]

At least one organization, Freight Data Systems, has introduced telecommuting primarily to reduce office space overhead and commuting costs. When the company experienced a growth rate which quickly expanded beyond what could be housed in the office, they decided that telecommuters with home terminals were the best solution to the office space problem.[15]

In summary, the findings of the few organizations which have introduced telecommuting indicates that they viewed telecommuting as a method to enrich jobs, employ the home-bound, and reduce office overhead and commuting costs. There were not empirical results reported by these organizations, but they seemed to consider the introduction of telecommuting successful and planned to continue the telecommuting programs.

4

The Research Model and Hypotheses

Despite the impression promoted by the popular press, few companies are actually conducting formal experiments with remote work options.[1] However, a larger number of companies are beginning to have an interest in investigating the potential of telecommuting.[2]

Several research studies on the effects of telecommunications on work and transportation in general have been done. However, "the limitations of such studies is that they do not examine the process by which that acceptance will occur or even the likelihood that it will."[3] These "human and organization factors will be the most significant problem areas—more so than technological factors."[4]

The problems of telecommuting relate directly to the organizational and behavioral effects of remote work. Such problems are concerned with the economic cost of providing the equipment needed to telecommute, the loss in face-to-face and social contact provided by the office, and the difficulties associated with managing remote workers. One of the key questions to the success of telecommuting concerns whether individuals perceive telecommuting as cost-beneficial to themselves and, hence, whether they would be willing to substitute some form of telecommuting for travel to work. A related question arises with respect to the attitudes and behaviors of managers. To what extent do managers perceive telecommuting as cost beneficial to the organization, and on what basis would they be willing to permit or encourage their employees to participate in telecommuting?[5]

This research focuses upon the human and organizational effects of using the telecommuting option to allow employees to work from their homes. As such, it will provide evidence about the desirability of telecommuting, whether the telecommuter's job is more or less enriched than that of his office counterpart, and whether individuals view telecommuting as cost-beneficial to themselves. Additionally, the organizational effects of telecommuting will be examined along with the perceptions of managers.

The research utilizes a model of the organizational and behavioral effects of telecommuting to guide a field experiment of employees from five organizations who telecommute from their homes. The remainder of this chapter discusses the development of the research model and presents the hypotheses to be specifically tested by the study.

The Research Model

The organizational and behavioral effects of telecommuting consist of many human, task, technical, and organizational variables.

> Given its [organizational behaviors] inherent complexity and enigmatic nature, one needs tools to unravel the mysteries, paradoxes, and apparent contradictions that present themselves in the everyday life of organizations. One tool is the conceptual framework or model. A model is a theory that indicates which factors (in an organization, for example) are most critical or important. It also shows how these factors are related; that is, which factors or combination of factors cause other factors to change. In a sense then, a model is a roadmap that can be used to make sense of the terrain of organizational behavior.[6]

A prerequisite to furthering and sharing research, especially exploratory research, is the use of an established framework or paradigm.[7] An established framework for investigating the organizational and behavioral effects of telecommuting does not exist; therefore, an appropriate framework was chosen from among several models used to investigate organizational change.

Leavitt[8] provides a model of the organization, figure 1, which is useful for organizational analysis. "One can view industrial organizations as complex systems in which at least four interacting variables loom especially large; task variables, structural variables, technological variables, and human variables."[9] Additionally, Leavitt's model of organizations, "in which STRUCTURE, TASK, PEOPLE, and

Figure 1. Organizational Change Model

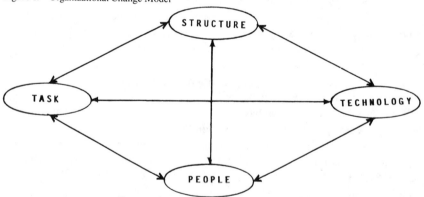

[Source: H. J. Leavitt, *Applied Organizational Change in Industry: Structural, Technological and Humanistic Approaches,* in J. C. March, ed., *Handbook of Organizations* (Chicago: Rand McNally, 1965)]

TECHNOLOGY are interrelated and mutually adjusting, indicates the complex nature of social systems."[10] The arrowheads indicate that the four variables are highly interdependent. Change in any one component usually results in an adjustment in others. Efforts to effect change, "whether they begin with people, technology, structure, or task, soon must deal with others."[11]

The introduction of new technological tools, computers, for example, may cause changes in structure (e.g., in the communication system or decision map of the organization), changes on actors (their numbers, skills, attitudes, and activities), and changes in performance or even definition of task, since some tasks may now become feasible of accomplishment for the first time, and others may become unnecessary.[12]

Leavitt's model was designed to be used in two ways. First, it can be used for storing and organizing knowledge extracted from the literature. The following sections use the model in this manner to describe each of the four components and the relevant literature associated with that component. Second, the model can be used as "a guide for diagnosing an organizational problem and choosing points of intervention for organizational change."[13] This second use of Leavitt's model will be employed to develop an adaptation according to the expected effects of telecommuting.

Using the Leavitt framework (figure 1), a model of the organizational effects of telecommuting was developed to guide this research and report the results. This

Figure 2. Organizational Effects of Telecommuting

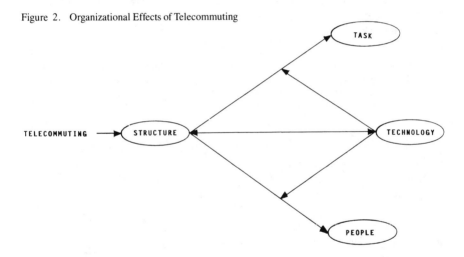

model, presented in figure 2, limits the relationships which will be investigated and serves as the basis for developing the hypotheses, instruments, and research approach.

The effects of telecommuting upon the task, people, and technological components are illustrated by the model. Additionally, the technologies used to implement telecommuting will have a moderating effect upon the degree to which the task and people components are changed by allowing employees to work from their homes. The components of the model and the associated hypotheses are discussed in detail in the following sections.

Structure

Structure refers to the "systems of communication, systems of authority (or other roles), and systems of work flow."[14] "Structure provides for the division of work and its coordination toward a common goal."[15]

Structural change has been the major transformation mechanism of the "classical" organizational theorist. The early structural approaches almost always mediated their activities through people to task. The concern of these structural approaches was with "appropriate divisions of labor and systems of authority."[16] One of the failings of early structural models was that the design of work was largely determined by task and technical variables which failed to adequately account for human and social needs.

A widespread approach to structural change is the mechanism of *decentralization*. Nilles indicates that telecommuting is a structural approach to organizational change in response to technical innovation. Telecommuting is an extension of decentralization which fragments the profit center concept into its ultimate extension — the individual working at home.

> Structural change toward decentralization should change the performance of certain organizational tasks and will also probably change the technology that is brought to bear and the nature, and/or motivation and attitudes of people in the organization. Any of these changes could presumably be consciously intended, or they could occur as unforeseen and often costly outcomes of efforts to change only one or two of the variables.[17]

The issues raised in the structural literature concern the effects of telecommuting upon the systems of communication, and management and control. Before examining this literature, the forms of structural change which can be introduced by telecommuting are discussed.

Forms of telecommuting. There are several forms of structural relocation of workers possible from telecommuting. Nilles[18] divides these dimension into four levels:

- Centralization: no relocation
- Fragmentation: relocation of coherent sub-units
- Dispersion: regional relocation of all organizational functions
- Diffusion: relocation of individual jobs to the workers' homes

Centralization is the working environment for most large organizations. "All administrative operations are located at a single site, with workers divided into functional groups according to their primary information product."[19] However, a restricted form of telecommuting could occur in an organization in which job locations remain centralized. Transportation can be traded for telecommunication by implementing applications such as teleconferencing and electronic mail.

Fragmentation occurs when an organization places coherent sub-units at remote locations. Two forms of fragmentation are present in many organizations. Branching, a familiar form of fragmentation, occurs in many banks. The branch is a miniature replica of the central office. Fragmentation occurs when specific functions such as marketing or data processing are located at a remote site.[20] A fragmented structure is also commonly referred to as a "satellite work center." The satellite work center is a relatively self-contained organizational division that is physically located away from the central office.

Dispersion occurs when the performance of most or all of the central office functions are performed at several regional locations. A dispersed organizational structure would place parts of the major organizational functions such as accounting, finance, and marketing at various regional locations called "neighborhood work centers." The separated functions would be linked together using telecommunications technology. An accountant, for example, would report to the nearest regional office and be able to carry out all the activities of the job even though other accountants are not physically located at that regional office.[21]

Finally, diffusion is the ultimate extension of telecommuting and involves individual employees working from their homes. This is the form of telecommuting which is specifically investigated by this research. Diffusion represents the most drastic change to the working environment and the most radical application of telecommuting.[22] Telecommuting from the home can range from one day a week to virtually full-time, where the employee rarely makes a trip to the central office. It is heavily communication dependent like the neighborhood work center, but it does not provide the social interaction that either a satellite or neighborhood work center would provide.[23]

Communication. The literature indicates that telecommuting should decrease upward, downward, and horizontal communication. An argument for telecommuting is typically based on the questionable assumption that electronics can substitute for face-to-face meetings (and therefore commuting) without altering the nature of communication. "Unfortunately, there is little evidence that direct substitution can occur — except in the simplest cases."[24] When there is a need for face-to-face communication, the only option currently available is for the employee to drive to the office.[25]

Hypotheses to test the effect of telecommuting upon communication are:

H1: Telecommuting individuals will spend less time communicating horizontally.

H2: Telecommuting individuals will spend less time communicating upward.

H3: Telecommuting individuals will spend less time communicating downward.

Several research studies also suggest that for programmed repetitive tasks, centralized communication structures are more efficient. The broad, open type of network with many channels and little differentiation seems to work better for more ill-structured tasks.[26] However, broad forms of communication networks appear to be difficult, if not impossible, in telecommuting situations; therefore, the nature of communication in a particular worker's task or job will likely determine the extent to which that worker can telecommute. The president of a software company interested in telecommuting expressed it this way: "What we're doing is complicated enough that it's better to be able to pull a guy into a meeting if necessary. *If* you have really clear design specifications, then telecommuting is very effective."[27] This effect of telecommuting upon communications is expressed as:

> H4:   Telecommuting will increase spatial-physical barriers which will reduce the telecommuter's ability to ask questions, talk with people, and access needed resource materials.

Management and control. Management and control of the remote telecommuter is very important if organizations are to accept the telecommuting concept.

> Probably the first thing to come to the managers' minds will be the question of how they can supervise the efforts of their subordinates. Is it reasonable to expect that the person who no longer reports to the office each day will climb out of bed with some semblance of regularity each morning and put in an honest day's work for his or her pay?[28]

Organizations and managers experimenting with telecommuting have developed several methods of insuring the adequate performance of a telecommuter. The methods may:

1. Limit telecommuters to people who have worked in-house and have gained the trust of the manager and the organization.
2. Require telecommuters to make frequent phone calls and/or occasional visits to the main office.
3. Monitor telecommuters through their telecommuting equipment.
4. Rely upon standards and piecework which place the responsibility for organizing and planning work time upon the telecommuters.

Unfortunately, none of these methods appears to deal effectively with the problems of remote management in all cases. First, determining who can be trusted to telecommute can lead to many unacceptable situations and legal issues. Second, reliance upon frequent phone calls and electronic supervision can create an atmosphere of oversupervision. Third, the management and control of the remote worker is not only a question of performance; it is also a question of evaluation.

> It violates a lot of traditional norms. . . . Many people who supervise others often base the quality of their employees' work on how they show up at the office — on time, dressed properly — and on how they deal with others.[29]

The general impression of the literature is that there will be less management and control of a remote worker than of a commuting worker. The hypothesis states:

> H5:   Telecommuting will result in a decrease in the amount of performance measurement and monitoring of the telecommuter.

Task

The task component refers "to industrial organizations' *raisons d'être*: the production of goods and services, including the large numbers of different but operationally meaningful subtasks that may exist in complex organizations."[30]

The literature on telecommuting as related to job tasks centers around determining what job characteristics are suitable for telecommuting and how they will be affected.

> The feasibility of substituting telecommuting for commuting to a central location depends upon the type of work the employee performs. If the employee is engaged in the physical creation or movement of goods (such as in a factory or in a trucking firm), then telecommuting clearly is not a viable alternative.[31]

While workers who are engaged in the physical creation and movement of goods cannot telecommute, recent trends in the western economies suggest that the proportion of these workers to workers who are not tied to the physical creation and transportation of goods is becoming smaller. Many of the workers whose jobs appear suited for telecommuting are classified as information workers.

Information workers whose primary job tasks involve collecting, summarizing, using, and communicating information occupied more than one-third of the total work force in 1970.[32] Figure 3 illustrates the hierarchical nature of the jobs of information workers.

Information workers work with a commodity (information) which can be easily transferred from one location to another using telecommunications technology. The most suitable information workers are therefore those who are experienced with telecommunications and computer technology and who are currently using computer terminals.[33]

The jobs of some types of managers, information analysts, computer professionals, and word processing operators are reported to be the most likely candidates for telecommuting. However, other research suggests that there are further restrictions on

Figure 3. Categories in the Information Subsystem

User Types	Job Types	Task Types
Users of Information	Executives Managers Field Professionals Bus. Professionals	Ill-Structured Tasks
Information Processors	Technical Professionals System Analysts Programmers Office Administrators	Semi-Structured Tasks
Information Collection and Entry	Secretaries Word Processors Clerical and Data Entry Clerks	Well-Structured Tasks

suitable telecommuting jobs due to constraints in the communication system and the difficulty in monitoring remote workers.

The restricted communication channels used by telecommuters suggest that their jobs should be less interdependent upon other workers in the organization. Telecommuters should possess either a low need to communicate with those in the organization, or be able to partition or "batch" their communication until they are in the office.[34] Either of these adjustments to a worker's job tasks suggests a decrease in task interdependence.

H6:   Telecommuting will reduce the job interdependence of the telecommuter.

Perhaps the greatest limitations placed upon job tasks by telecommuting stem from the difficulty in managing and monitoring the remote worker. Some of the literature suggests that this constraint will necessitate job tasks which are characterized as project oriented with long term completion dates which have well defined deliverables and well defined milestones.[35] Other reports suggest that the problem of remote management will produce contractual work where workers are paid by fees rather than wages.[36] In either case, the effect will be that a telecommuter's job will contain fewer job tasks.

H7:   Telecommuting will reduce the job tasks of the telecommuter.

Vallee[37] reports that using telecommunications to communicate works "well for tasks such as exchanging information, giving orders or generating ideas." However, tasks which involve "complex interpersonal communication, such as bargaining and negotiation or even getting to know someone, seem to be more difficult."[38] It would therefore seem that job tasks which rely upon these types of communication would be more complex in a telecommuting situation and the job would be more ill-structured due to an inability to get adequate clarification of the required tasks and how these tasks coincide with the overall organizational mission.

H8: Telecommuting will make the telecommuter's job more uncertain (ill-structured).

People

The people component refers primarily to the motivations, attitudes, performance, and feelings of the people in the organization. A large amount of investigation by industrial psychologists has been directed toward the workers in organizations. Focusing upon job satisfaction, motivation, training, and performance, "research in this area has been reasonably successful, both in terms of increasing scholarly understanding of the processes at work and in developing practical applications."[39]

Changes to the organizational structure by the introduction of telecommuting is expected to directly affect the people component. An understanding of the effects of telecommuting upon the people component is important to the development of methods to successfully introduce telecommuting. "By changing human behavior, it is argued, one can cause the creative invention of new tools, or one can cause modifications in structure."[40]

The literature concerning the behavioral effects of telecommuting is divided into the effects of telecommuting upon organizational commitment and relationships, performance, job satisfaction, and attitudes.

Organizational commitment and relationships. The literature related to organizational commitment indicates that telecommuting may reduce a worker's identification with the organization and also decrease organizational loyalty. Additionally, it is predicted that telecommuting will increase a telecommuter's identification with neighbors and professional peers and result in an ability to market his talents to several companies. The ability of specialists to market themselves among several organizations over a wide geographic area may further undermine organizational identity[41] and "weaken ties between employees and their companies."[42]

H9: Telecommuting will adversely affect the telecommuter's individual organizational behavior.

Organizational relationships are also predicted to be adversely affected by telecommuting. Research on using telecommunications indicates that remote communication is more focused and that differences in cultural background, organizational commitment, and goals and objectives are harder to discern. The limitations of the restricted communication channels "may not build cohesiveness"[43] and may result in a deterioration in organizational relationships. Relations with co-workers can be expected to suffer. One word processing operator who tried telecommuting for two years and then returned to the office stated that, "My old colleagues didn't think to include me as much. It got kind of lonely."[44]

> H10: Telecommuting will adversely affect the telecommuter's intragroup organizational behavior.

Some reports suggest that the inability of managers to supervise remotely will have a negative influence upon managerial relationships. Telecommuting is suggested to be "negative in terms of promotion. Most companies still take the attitude, 'out of sight, out of mind.' If you're not clearly visible at headquarters, you probably won't gain promotion."[45]

> H11: Telecommuting will adversely affect the telecommuter's vertical organizational behavior.

Performance. While performance must be viewed as a composite criterion including many variables such as job effort, satisfaction, organizational relationships, and role communication, the effect of telecommuting appears extremely positive if one accepts what is reported in the popular press. In some preliminary studies, telecommuters consisting largely of programmers and system analysts all indicated that they were "one to three times more productive working at home," and "would never consider returning to an office-based, salaried job."[46] Part-time data processors were reported to put in "five concentrated hours a day" on the average and "produce a week's work in less time than full-time office workers."[47]

> Where productivity data was available, it was very encouraging. One company reported an *average* increase of 100 percent in productivity for programmer/analysts working at home.[48]

These claims of increased performance are inconsistent with the other indications of decreased communication, management and control, and restricted jobs tasks. Therefore, this research will test to see if performance is adversely affected by telecommuting instead of testing to see if telecommuting will increase performance.

> H12 : Telecommuting will adversely effect the telecommuter's performance, turnover, and absenteeism.

Job satisfaction. The effect of telecommuting on job satisfaction is largely unknown and inconclusive. While there are several reports of increased job satisfaction as a result of telecommuting, there are also several indications of decreased satisfaction. For example, telecommuting professionals have indicated that stress was a condition of both office and at-home work. Increased stress at home appears due to a greater need for self-discipline and the necessity to structure the working environment. The need to structure the home to accommodate both work and family activities occasionally creates conflicts between the at-home work schedule and the families of telecommuters.[49]

Additionally, a representative of Working Women, an organization in Los Angeles for office workers, predicts that telecommuting may cause more problems than it solves for office workers.

> Clerical workers don't have decision-making powers about the kind of work they do. Work satisfaction is lower than for professionals because most clerical work is routine, and the pay is much lower. Clerical workers at home may feel even more isolation and less job satisfaction. Because they're isolated, they may also lack any resource for solving problems or mediating grievances. . . the office may become a 24-hour work place[50]

H13: Telecommuting will decrease the telecommuter's job satisfaction.

Attitude. A final concern of the effect of telecommuting upon the people component is attitude. Attitudes of telecommuters, managers and co-workers about telecommuting will "present the main problems in achieving its overall acceptance."[51]

> Company managers will have to accept that its not an embarrassment to tell a client that an employee is working at home. Bosses will have to trust that their workers aren't out playing nine holes of golf instead of meeting deadlines.

The changes in attitude of telecommuters, managers, and co-workers that occur when a remote work alternative is implemented is unknown. The hypotheses related to the changes in attitudes of telecommuters, managers, and co-workers will test to determine if attitudes deteriorate.

H14: Telecommuting will have a negative effect on the telecommuter's attitude toward working at home.

H15: Telecommuting will have a negative effect on the attitude of the telecommuter's manager toward working at home.

H16: Telecommuting will have a negative effect on the attitude of the telecommuter's co-workers toward working at home.

Technology

Leavitt refers to the technology component as any "direct problem solving inventions like work-measurement techniques or computers or drill presses."[52] Leavitt classifies both machines and programs in the technical category. This research limits the technological component to the computer and telecommunication tools which are used to allow organizational employees to work from their homes. As such, the technology component is to moderate (decrease or increase) the effects which telecommuting may have upon the task and people components.

The model used in this research illustrates that technology will not only be affected by telecommuting but will be a strong moderator of the effects of telecommuting on the other components. The literature on the moderating role of technology indicates that the use of telecommunications and office automation technology to make telecommuting possible will likely have a variety of organizational and behavioral effects on the other components of the research model.

> The introduction of computers, or other pieces of "big ticket" technology, may change the jobs of employees and the satisfaction they derive from their job [the people component]; it may force new, centralized, standardized ways of communicating [the structural component]; or it may realign strategic constituencies and affect the goal mix of the organization [the task component]. The administrator, therefore, needs to anticipate possible negative impacts that such technological changes may bring.[53]

For example, some research has suggested that an excessive dependence upon telecommunications could undermine the more personal, and perhaps critical, aspects of business relationships.

> Contrary to Bell System ads, the system is definitely not the solution. Teleconferencing is the child of engineering, so it is perhaps not surprising that an undue emphasis has been placed on the technology of teleconferencing — often at the expense of social and organizational structures to support communication.[54]

In another example, Uhlig[55] reports that telecommunication systems tend to produce a leveling effect on the organizational hierarchy by allowing people to bypass the traditional communication barriers in an organization.

One of the most extensive experiments concerning the effects of using telecommunications to communicate in a business environment was conducted by the Business Planning Group of Bell Canada[56] using the NLS (On Line System) developed by the Augmentation Research Center at Stanford Research Institute. Leduc concluded that:

- The telecommunications system was used extensively for communication between superiors and subordinates.

- It was not used much for an exchange of messages stating a personal point of view or the expression of feelings about an event or a situation which was not job-related.
- It was not used only in a crisis or an emergency, but continuously for routine administrative tasks.
- It was being used successfully for project management.
- It was used extensively for the exchange of information between professionals in the same group or in different organizations.

This study also indicated that using telecommunications to communicate enhanced the flexibility in the choice of working hours. This is supported by Vallee[57] which also found that forty percent of the teleconferencing sessions occurred outside of normal working hours. The ability of a telecommunication system to enhance the flexibility of working hours appears to be a "consequence of using any effective computer communication system."[58]

The literature supports the contention that computer and telecommunications technology can moderate the effects of telecommuting upon many of the model's components and variables. The hypotheses to test this moderating role of technology are:

H17: Use of telecommunications and computer technology will have a positive correlation with the amount of horizontal, upward, and downward communication.

H18: Use of telecommunications and computer technology will have a positive correlation with the amount of performance measurement and monitoring of the telecommuter.

H19: Use of telecommunications and computer technology will have a positive correlation with the telecommuter's job interdependence (work flow).

H20: Use of telecommunications and computer technology will correlate with fewer changes to the job tasks of the telecommuter.

H21: Use of telecommunications and computer technology will correlate with a reduction in the complexity (ill-structure) of the telecommuter's job.

H22: Use of telecommunications and computer technology will correlate with the telecommuter having a better attitude toward working at home.

H23: Use of telecommunications and computer technology will correlate with the manager of the telecommuter having a better attitude toward working at home.

H24: Use of telecommunications and computer technology will correlate with the co-workers of the telecommuter having a better attitude toward working at home

H25: Use of telecommunications and computer technology will correlate with higher job satisfaction by the telecommuter.

In summary, the first set of hypotheses, H1-H16, will provide evidence of the organizational and behavioral effects of allowing workers to telecommute from their homes. The second set of hypotheses, H17-H25, are used to test the commonly held belief that technology can be used to moderate the negative organizational and behavioral effects of working at home, thereby making telecommuting a viable alternative.

5

Research Approach

The research approach is designed to test the hypotheses presented in the last chapter and to provide preliminary information about the organizational and behavioral effects of telecommuting. To date, information concerning the effects of telecommuting have been limited to passive observations and surveys of telecommuters. The research approach used in this study extends that knowledge by using an experimental design to actively monitor telecommuters, their managers, and co-workers over a six month period. The results are compared against a matched control group of workers who are not working at home in order to test the causal propositions stated in the hypotheses.

Experimental Design Considerations

Use of experimental designs became systematized during the past century for testing causal propositions. Initially the experimental designs emphasized the physical control of conditions which might confound or obscure the expected outcomes. Such procedures as isolation, insulation, sterilization, and soundproofing were frequently used to accomplish environmental control. Later as biological research moved out of the laboratory into the open field, the theory of experimental control using randomized assignment of treatments emerged.

> In agricultural work the emphasis is usually on whether a new practice or technique will increase the yield per acre. Note that, unlike Pascal's work in physics, this problem implies a particular single cause, the effects of which the researcher would like to evaluate. To do this, he or she creates different agricultural plots and deliberately assigns to each a different type of seed, fertilizer, method of raking, or whatever is under investigation.[1]

Telecommuting is classified as the treatment or independent variable. It is the new practice or technique whose effects are of interest. Strictly defined, an individual receives this treatment if he is scheduled to work during regular working hours from his home either full-time or part-time.

The possible effects of telecommuting are referred to as outcomes or dependent variables. These outcome variables span a wide range of organizational and behavioral variables due to the exploratory nature of the study. They include measures of communications, spatial-physical effects, work flows, organizational commitment, use of technology, job satisfaction, job task changes, performance, and attitude.

To infer the effects of the telecommuting, the outcomes of telecommuters are compared with individuals who are not working at home. Differences found among the groups are attributed to telecommuting. The degree of confidence that is placed upon the inferences is dependent upon the method used to assign the individuals to either the telecommuting or comparison group.

The most powerful and preferred type of assignment method would randomly place selected individuals into either the telecommuting or comparison group.

Randomized experiments are characterized by the use of initial random assignment for inferring treatment-caused change. It is more difficult to assign individuals or larger social groups to treatments at random than it is to assign agricultural plots. It is also more difficult to assign individuals to treatments at random in field settings than in laboratory settings. The field researcher is often a guest at the sites where he or she works while the laboratory researcher has almost total control over the setting and acts as the respondent's host.[2]

The choice of the experimental setting therefore limits the degree to which individuals can be assigned to the experimental groups. A field experiment virtually eliminates the use a randomized experiment. Therefore, a critical decision in choosing an experimental design was whether the study should be carried out in a field or laboratory setting.

The use of a laboratory setting seemed inappropriate for an exploratory study of the effects of telecommuting. Little, if any, empirical evidence that could be tested in a laboratory was of interest. Additionally, the artificial construction of a true work environment within which subjects could work was impractical. Therefore, a field or organizational setting for the experiment was chosen since a true working environment could be utilized along with actual organizational employees.

The loss of control due to the choice of a field experiment has a major impact on the ability to make causal statements concerning the results. Control[3] in the sense of this research design refers to the researcher's ability to determine:

1. which individuals receive a particular treatment at a particular time.
2. the situation in which the experiments are being conducted so as to keep out extraneous forces.
3. the degree to which the experimental process is hidden or unknown to the participants (e.g. eliminating the Hawthorne effect).

The most serious limitation caused by choosing a field setting was the inability to randomly determine which workers would be allowed to telecommute. Lacking the ability to randomly assign individuals to this treatment placed the study within a group of experimental designs termed quasi-experiments. These are "experiments that have treatments, outcome measures, and experimental units, but do not use random assignment to create the comparisons from which treatment-caused change is inferred."[4] Comparisons in these types of designs depend upon nonequivalent groups. That is, the comparison groups will differ from each other in ways besides participation or nonparticipation in telecommuting. Interpreting the results from the quasi-experimental design must therefore be concerned with separating the effects of the telecommuting treatment from the effects due to the initial selection nonequivalence between the comparison groups.

A second negative consequence which resulted from the choice of a field experiment was the inability to keep out extraneous forces. The size of the sample was determined by the willingness of organizations within a small geographical area to participate in a risky and perhaps costly flirtation with a new and innovative concept — telecommuting. As a result, the sample size was much smaller than would have been possible in the laboratory. Additionally, "In the laboratory, one is more likely to be able to implement parametric studies in which many levels of a treatment are manipulated across a wide range."[5] In this field experiment, the number of days that an individual telecommuter worked at home was largely beyond the control of the experimenter and varied from a few days per week to full-time.

The third consequence of the field experiment was that the subjects in the experiment clearly understood the purpose and extent of the experiment. It is impossible to hide the fact that telecommuting experiments are being conducted. Therefore, there is a real possibility that the "Hawthorne effect" may produce some of the observed outcomes rather than the treatment, telecommuting.

The Experimental Design

The experimental design was constructed to overcome many of the problems mentioned in the previous section. A nonequivalent group design, in which responses of a treatment group and a comparison group are measured before and after a treatment, was used. The nonequivalent group design gathered data before the experiment began (pretelecommuting period) and at three and six months after the treatment group began telecommuting (post-test period).

The following diagram illustrates this design.

	Pretelecommuting		Post-test 3 Mos.	6 Mos.
Experimental Group	O	X	O	O
Control Group	O		O	O

The first row represents the telecommuting participants, and the second row represents the comparison control group. The X indicates the treatment, telecommuting from the home; an O represents the collection of data using structured interviews, questionnaires, and work records.

This experimental design is an extension of a generally interpretable non-equivalent control group design which Cook and Campbell refer to as "The Untreated Control Group with Pretest and Post-test."[6] The extension involves obtaining a second set of post-test measures six months after the subjects began telecommuting. Cook and Campbell's design involves only a single post-test.

Prior or pretelecommuting measurements of the outcome variables obtained from both comparison groups provides an estimate of the degree of initial non-equivalence between the groups. Post-test measurements of the outcome variables taken three and six months after the telecommuters begin working from their homes are adjusted by the pretelecommuting measures to separate the effects of telecommuting from those pertaining to the initial nonequivalence between the comparison groups.

The use of two post-test measures provided information as to the effects of time upon telecommuters. The idea that an individual might be able to work at home for a short while but be unable to cope with the lack of communication, social interaction, and organizational commitment for a long period was investigated by using two post-test measures over a six month period.

Additionally, the use of two post-test measures helped overcome the possibility of the "Hawthorne Effect." Individuals who were selected to telecommute were generally excited and very positive about the possibility of working at home. It was feared that these individuals might artificially overcome negative influences of telecommuting so that the telecommuting programs could continue and possibly expand. The ability of individuals to mitigate negative influences over a relatively long period of time would be more difficult than over a short period. Therefore, if negative outcomes of telecommuting were to show up during the six month data gathering period and not during the three month period, this could be due to the time effect of telecommuting or to the dissipation of the Hawthorne effect.

Causal Connections

The issue of demonstrating "causal connections" between telecommuting and the outcome variables was so affected by the choice of a field experiment that a brief discussion of "cause" is necessary.

In this research, a causal connection between the treatment, telecommuting, and an outcome variable is defined in the general sense of everyday language. The definition of this general use of "causation" is defined by Cook and Campbell[7] and is summarized in the following statements.

- General causal assertions are meaningful even when the underlying details of the cause-effect relationship are not known.
- The effects of general causal assertions can be the result of multiple causes.
- General causal assertions, because they are contingent on many other conditions and causes, are fallible and hence probabilistic.
- Dependable intermediate mediational units are involved in general causal assertions.
- Effects are seen to follow general causal assertions in time.
- Some general causal assertions can be reversed, with cause and effect interchangeable.
- The paradigmatic assertion in causal relationships is that the manipulation of a cause will result in the manipulation of an effect.

This definition of cause provides important preliminary information about the organization and behavioral effects of telecommuting. However, additional research will be needed before strong causal connections between telecommuting and the outcome variables can be extended to individuals, jobs, and organizational settings not investigated in this study. The next chapter discusses the sample of participants along with their organizations and jobs.

6

Sample and Classification

After choosing a field experiment, the researcher engaged in an effort to identify and select a sample of potential telecommuters from local organizations. Measuring the set of outcome variables required personal observation coupled with a rather extensive set of questionnaires and interviews. Thus, the telecommuters had to be chosen from organizations within a limited geographic area in the upper Midwest. The search started with one organization and three telecommuters.

Organizations

The first organization chosen for the experiment actually chose the researcher by expressing to the MIS Research Center at the University of Minnesota a desire to experiment with the concept of telecommuting . This organization, labeled Company 1, had permitted an employee within the data processing group to work at home. The results from this initial test proved encouraging. Additional reports from Continental Illinois National Bank and Trust of Chicago on the successful use of telecommuting word processing operators indicated that telecommuting might be introduced in their word processing function to reduce costs.

In order to acquire additional organizations and telecommuters, a series of discussion groups were organized through the MIS Research Center. Over fifty letters were mailed to individuals employed in organizations seeking their participation in the discussion group. Twenty-eight individuals representing twelve organizations responded to this letter. Additionally, several organizations which had introduced telecommuting were personally invited to attend and present a short description of their experiences.

The purpose of the discussion groups was to explore the issues of telecommuting and to locate organizations which would be interested in participating in the telecommuting experiment. The meetings produced a list of issues and questions about introducing telecommuting. This list centered almost solely on the behavioral and organizational implications of telecommuting. The issues and questions developed by the discussion groups were used in the development of the interviews and questionnaires to be administered during the experiment.

Several outcomes which would affect procuring a sample of organizations and telecommuters also resulted from the discussion group. First, the desire on the part of the researcher to limit the telecommuting experiments to a single job class, thereby eliminating confounding influences of job differences, would be impractical. No other organization was willing to participate in a telecommuting experiment limited to word processing operators. Second, while all of the participants expressed great interest in the concept of telecommuting, few were willing to be one of the first organizations to directly experiment with the idea in a non-proprietary fashion. Finally, three of the five organizations willing to participate in the experiment would allow only a single employee to telecommute actively.

Company 2 was one of the organizations which agreed to experiment with telecommuting on a relatively large scale basis. Having had some prior experience with telecommuting, this company anticipated introducing a telecommuting plan for a division that was in the process of being relocated. The relocation would be a burden for some of the employees, and the variety of jobs performed at the division were viewed as appropriate for telecommuting. The initial plan was to select thirteen to fourteen employees from three areas for participation in a pilot program. The actual implementation included eleven participants. One of the individuals never participated due to a promotion and transfer. The actual number of telecommuters involved in the pilot project of Company 2 was ten.

Company 3 was preparing to allow an individual who had several small children to begin working from home. This individual was highly experienced and valuable to the organization, but she had determined that priority would be given to spending the next several years raising her children. In order to retain this individual, the organization made plans to introduce telecommuting.

Company 4 decided to introduce telecommuting to accommodate the financial needs of an individual who also had several children. The summer months would necessitate a babysitter for both the preschool children and those who were out of school. This would almost completely offset the financial reward of working. The organization was interested in the concept of telecommuting and agreed to allow the individual to telecommute for the summer. Their experiment was planned to last only three months with a possible extension for another three months. The results of this organization's experiments were included in the study even though it was not extended and lasted only three months.

Company 5 was interested in telecommuting to solve a shortage of office space. One of the operating divisions of Company 5 had grown considerably and was continuing to grow. Lacking adequate space, an employee was selected to work at home after initial job training at the central site. The individual shared the space of another employee on his days in the office.

This group of organizations and telecommuters comprised the experimental treatment group. As mentioned, selection of who would telecommute and what organizations would participate was beyond the control of the researcher.

Organization	Number of Telecommuters
Company 1	3
Company 2	10
Company 3	1
Company 4	1
Company 5	1
Total	16

Job Types

Restricting the types of jobs performed by the telecommuters would have eliminated many confounding and contingent causes of outcomes. However, this limitation was not feasible due to the newness of the concept of telecommuting and the differing needs of participating organizations. Therefore, a variety of job types is represented by the sample. The advantage of this variety was that it provided the research with additional preliminary information about the contingent influences of job types on telecommuting. The disadvantage was that the variety of job types, when coupled with the relatively small sample size, created a larger than anticipated variance in the outcome measures thereby obscuring some causal relationships.

The jobs represented in the sample include word processing operator, editor, text developer, programming developer, programmer/analyst, and programmer designer. Figure 4 shows the number of telecommuters by job in each organization.

Figure 4. Job and Organizational Matrix of the Telecommuters

Jobs	Organizations					Totals
	1	2	3	4	5	
Word Processing Operator	3	—	—	—	—	3
Editor	—	2	—	—	—	2
Text Developer	—	2	—	—	—	2
Programming Developer	—	3	—	—	—	3
Programmer/Analyst	—	—	1	1	1	3
Program Designer	—	3	—	—	—	3
Totals	3	10	1	1	1	16

Word Processing Operator

The job with the most structured tasks was word processing operator. The word processing center was centralized into a single location in this organization. Work from the entire organization was sent to this central site for processing. The tasks included the typing of dictation, stored letters, statistical tables and charts, and handwritten documents. The employees were rotated on a daily basis among these different tasks to increase their work variety. The percentage of time typically devoted to each of these tasks was largely determined by the amount of work received by the word processing center. During the experimental period, this breakdown was approximately:

Dictation	40%
Stored Letters	20%
Tables and Charts	20%
Handwritten Documents	20%

Some individuals in the word processing center had additional responsibilities such as receiving and assigning work, and the storing, printing, and distribution of documents.

Editor

The job of editor operated in a project environment which developed multimedia educational programs. Approximately sixty percent of the time in this job was concerned with content, style, and format editing of multimedia materials produced by the project teams. The tasks involved in this effort included ensuring that the materials were accurate, consistent, and followed specific objectives. This required checking content, style, reading level, spelling, and grammatical construction. Thirty percent of the job required the direct composition and production of textual material including format plans, cover designs, binding requirements, and proofing typeset material. Approximately eight percent of the job was spent communicating with project teams, training new employees, and documenting the resources used in the editing process. The remaining portion of the job pertained to evaluating the contractual production of materials and overall product quality.

Text Developer

The job of text developer involved the development of textual material. Approximately sixty percent of the time was spent in the actual writing of text materials including introductions, exercises, test items, and user guides. This activity included developing the strategy to be used in the text, organization of the text, and application of techniques of instructional technology to design the content of the text. Twenty percent of the job was spent assessing the feasibility of the project and obtaining contact information from experts. Ten percent of the job was concerned with coordinating and communicating with other members of the project team, and another ten percent was used to ensure the proper evaluation and quality of the textual product.

Programming Developer

Programming developers perform jobs related to the development of computer-assisted instructional materials. Approximately fifty percent of the job involved the design, development, and programming of computer packages. Thirty percent of the job was concerned with training personnel and interacting with knowledgeable experts and other project team members. The remaining twenty percent of the time was spent conducting research and ensuring high quality products.

Programmer/Analyst

Programmer/analysts also operated in project oriented environments which developed new application software for the financial and business needs of the companies. Approximately sixty-five percent of the programmer/analyst's job directly focused upon the design, development, specification, and programming of these new applications. Twenty percent of the job concerned interacting with customers and coordinating with project team members to ensure proper design and specification of the project. The remaining fifteen percent of the job involved keeping abreast of current developments, programming methods, and computer hardware.

Program Designer

The job of program designer concerned the design and coordination of team efforts in the development of projects. At least twenty-five percent of this job involved ascertaining and coordinating the customer requirements, job specifications, schedules, and budgets of the proposed projects. Another twenty-five percent of the job entailed developing the specifications of the design which would be used by the project team members in their development of the project. Coordinating the project effort among the various members and monitoring the development required approximately twenty percent of the designer's job. Final evaluation and follow-up of the finished product involved ten percent of the job. Ten percent of the job was also involved in an analysis of the resources needed to accomplish the project, and another ten percent was used for additional training.

The designer's job contained the most ill-structured tasks involved in the sample. Designers served as functional project leaders who coordinated and monitored the development projects and ensured proper progress and adherence to design specifications. The job required a substantial amount of interaction, but also involved long periods of concentrated mental intensive work. One-half of the time on the job was generally spent communicating and interacting with groups, individuals, customers, and peers; the other one-half of the time was involved with intense mental paper and pencil work analyzing, designing, and reporting the project and budgets.

The job types involved in the sample ranged from the structured tasks of the word processing operator to the project leader role of the designer. The amount of communication and interaction necessary to the performance of the jobs was dependent upon the structuredness of the job. The word processing operators required very little communication and interaction while approximately fifty percent or more of designers' jobs involved interaction with other individuals. All jobs except word processing operated in a project team environment and therefore required some degree of coordination with other team members. Additionally, many of the jobs required that some amount of time be spent either training others or enhancing their own knowledge.

Forming a group whose outcome measures could be compared to the outcome measures of the telecommuters was necessary to try and isolate the effects of telecommuting from those of maturation, organizational change, and other extraneous influences which could not be controlled. This group of comparison individuals would comprise the control group.

Control Group

The control group consisted of individuals who volunteered to complete the interview and questionnaires in parallel with the group of telecommuters. The measures obtained from the control group were compared to those obtained from the group of telecommuters. This comparison attempted to isolate the effects of telecommuting from those effects which were uncontrollable and not a result of telecommuting. For example, one of the organizations began preparations for a divisional reorganization during the later part of the experiment. Without an appropriate control group with which to compare the outcome measure of the telecommuters, the outcomes could be attributed to the reorganization plan as well as to telecommuting. To be able to make valid comparisons, the control group would have to resemble the telecommuting group in as many factors as practicable except for the treatment — telecommuting.

Individuals in the control group were matched as closely as possible to individuals in the telecommuting group. A control individual belonged to the same organization and performed the same job as a telecommuting participant. Additionally, an attempt was made to select control individuals who were viewed by their supervisors as likely telecommuting candidates. This match was performed so that the same choice decisions which went into selecting the group of telecommuters would be used to select the group of controls. That is, if a supervisor selected a telecommuter because he worked well alone, was trustworthy, and had several years of experience, the best control individual should also possess these characteristics. This level of matching was done by asking the supervisors who were responsible for selecting the telecommuters, "If the person you asked to be involved in the telecommuting study had declined to participate, who was the next person you would have asked?" This type of matching was only possible for the eleven employees in Companies 2 and 5 where they intended to select telecommuters from existing employees and were not attempting to meet the needs of a specific individual.

Company 1 decided to select telecommuters from the home-bound labor force to test the feasibility of utilizing this segment of the labor market for word processing operators. They did not plan to allow any of their presently employed operators to work from their homes. The control individuals from Company 1 were selected from the word processing central site. They were individuals who, in age, sex, and education, matched the telecommuters from Company 1. However, the control subjects differed from the telecommuters in that the telecommuters had no experience with word processing while the control subjects averaged over three years of word processing experience. Inexperienced telecommuters were intentionally selected by Company 1 to test the feasibility of hiring this type of worker to telecommute.

Companies 3 and 4 had specific individuals in mind whom they were seeking to accommodate by affording them the telecommuting option. These two organizations would not have asked other individuals to telecommute. The control group was matched by job, age, sex, job experience, and education with the telecommuting individuals from these two organizations.

A group of sixteen individuals was selected to participate in the experiment as control subjects. Measurements from the resulting sample of sixteen controls was obtained in the pretelecommuting round of observations. Subsequently, one of the control individuals asked to be excused from further participation due to excessive job demands, and a second control individual was transferred out of the operating division. This resulted in a sample of fourteen control individuals matched with sixteen telecommuting participants for the two post-test periods.

This imbalance in sample size affected the degree to which the control and telecommuting groups were matched. However, the loss of these individuals did not exhaust the control measurements for any one job type. It did, unfortunately, exhaust the control measurements for two of the companies since both of the abstaining control subjects were from organizations that were studying only one telecommuter.

7

Data Collection

A data collection procedure was developed to test the hypotheses and provide additional information concerning the effects of time on telecommuters. A series of questionnaires and interviews were administered to the telecommuters and control individuals over a six month period. This chapter describes the data collection procedure and presents a description of the techniques and instruments used.

Data Collection Procedure

Information was collected from the telecommuters and control subjects before the telecommuters began working at home. This pretelecommuting period of data collection served three purposes. First, it provided useful information which was compared to post-test observations and measures to ascertain the effects of telecommuting. Second, it provided the researcher with an orientation into the organization and the various jobs performed. Finally, it would produced an organizational testing of the various questions used in the structured interviews and questionnaires to determine their applicability across organizations and job settings.

The first part of the pretelecommuting data gathering period involved interviewing the managers of individuals selected to telecommute. The managers were asked for permission to contact the telecommuters and also helped in selecting the appropriate control individuals. Following this interview, the telecommuters and control subjects were contacted to set up an interview and were mailed letters of introduction.

The pretelecommuting data collection period gathered information using the Pretelecommuting Interview (Appendix A, Exhibit 1) and two questionnaires: Attitude Towards Working at Home (Appendix A, Exhibit 2), and the Minnesota Satisfaction Questionnaire.[1] These questionnaires will be discussed in greater detail in the next section.

The post-test data collection periods (three months and six months after the telecommuters began working at home) used the Working at Home Interview (Appendix A, Exhibit 3), the Minnesota Satisfaction Questionnaire, and the Working at Home Questionnaire (Appendix A, Exhibit 4).

Instruments and Techniques

The data gathering instruments and techniques are discussed in this section. These include two structured interviews and three questionnaires which were used to collect data from the telecommuters and control individuals. In addition, two interviews were used to gather the data from the managers and co-workers of the telecommuters.

Pretelecommuting Interview

The Pretelecommuting Interview (Appendix A, Exhibit 1) consisted of three sections: an introduction; a series of general open-ended questions to gather information concerning the individual and his or her job; and a set of fixed response questions concerning communication, spatial-physical barriers, work flows, task complexity, organizational behavior, and use of technology. The questions directly corresponded with the hypotheses presented and were developed specifically for this research. Each of the categories of questions related to one of the hypothesis.

The section of fixed response questions was administered as an interview for the pretelecommuting data gathering period. Feedback concerning the appropriateness of the questions and response categories was used to construct the first section of the Working at Home Questionnaire (Appendix A, Exhibit 3) which was completed in the two post-test periods. These questions are discussed below under the Working at Home Questionnaire section.

Attitude towards Working at Home Questionnaire

The Attitude Towards Working at Home Questionnaire (Appendix A, Exhibit 2) measured changes in job tasks and attitude towards working at home in the pretelecommuting data gathering period. The questionnaire consisted of three sections.

Section 1 in the Attitude Questionnaire contained a list of the tasks derived from performance evaluation factors used to rate employees. Individuals in each job category completed a questionnaire that contained only the tasks specific to their job and were asked to indicate the number of hours per week spent on each task. The participants were also asked to indicate the number of hours per week spent on each of the tasks, the amount of time spent working alone, and the amount of time spent working at home.

The second section measured a participant's attitude and intention to work at home. These questions were developed using the procedures described by Ajzen and Fishbein.[2]

The third section of the Attitude Questionnaire was concerned with demographic questions. Information was obtained concerning length of employment, age, sex, education, number of people living at home, children, and commuting distance.

The first two sections of this questionnaire were later incorporated into the Working at Home Questionnaire to be administered during the post-test data gathering periods. The third section which obtained demographic information was not used in the Working at Home Questionnaire since these characteristics would remain constant over the experimental period.

Job Satisfaction Questionnaire

The long form of the Minnesota Satisfaction Questionnaire was completed by the telecommuters and control subjects during all three measurement periods to determine changes in job satisfaction which could be attributable to telecommuting.

The Minnesota Satisfaction Questionnaire[3] is organized into a set of intrinsic and extrinsic scales. Twenty factors are measured by the questionnaire. Each factor is measured by five questions using a five-point rating scale, and respondents were asked to rate each item according to how they felt about that item in their present job.

Working at Home Interview

After gathering the initial data, an interview procedure was developed to elicit supporting subjective observations from the telecommuters about their experiences with working at home. This Working at Home Interview (Appendix A, Exhibit 3) utilized a "critical incident" approach whereby the participant was asked to give specific incidents in which working at home had affected some aspect of his work or behavior. It was administered three and six months after the telecommuters began working at home. The responses obtained from these incidents were important to developing an understanding of the causal effects of telecommuting and explaining the resulting outcomes.

Working at Home Questionnaire

The Working at Home Questionnaire (Appendix A, Exhibit 4) was developed from the Pretelecommuting Interview and Attitude Towards Working at Home Questionnaire. It was administered three and six months after the telecommuters began working at home.

The most significant difference between the Pretelecommuting Interview questions and the Working at Home Questionnaire concerned the alteration of the response scales. During the pretelecommuting interview, the participants were asked to give their responses along a nine-point scale anchored by the percentages of time spent doing a particular activity, or the extent of their commitment to the organization or job. This response scale produced considerable frustration and unreliable responses. Additionally, the need for a "no time" response became apparent. The Working at Home Questionnaire corrected these deficiencies by modifying the response scale to a ten-point scale anchored by the words: NONE, LITTLE, SOME, MODERATE, CONSIDERABLE, and EXTENSIVE. Responses were considered to be ordinal and were scored using the numbers 0-9. A blank response was considered missing.

Several changes to the questions were also incorporated into the Working at Home Questionnaire. A specific time frame reference within the questions was established and some questions were clarified.

The first section of the Working at Home Questionnaire corresponds to the third section of the Pretelecommuting Interview. This section contains six categories of questions which were developed from a combination of input from implementers of telecommuting, prior literature, discussion group questions, and organizational literature.

The first category of questions concerns the amount of communication the individual telecommuter or control subject normally encountered in his or her job. These questions are based upon the classification of Katz and Kahn[4] and are located in Category 1.00 of the first section of the Working at Home Questionnaire. Categories 2.00, 3.00, 4.00, and 5.00 in this section contain questions respectively on the spatial-physical barriers, work flows, task complexity, and organizational behavior of the telecommuters and the control individuals. These questions were adapted from questions developed by Melcher[5] to understand the determinants of behavior in complex organizations. Category 6.00 of the questionnaire concerns an individual's use of the computer and telephone in performing his job for upward, downward, and horizontal communication.

Performance, Turnover, and Absenteeism

Performance measures were gathered from existing work records and from the third section of the Working at Home Questionnaire. This section contains a list of the tasks taken from performance evaluations in each of the job categories set against a response matrix. The participant was instructed to place within the matrix an "I" to represent how important a specific task is to his job, and then to place an "E" in the matrix to indicate how effective he felt he was in the accomplishment of that task. A ten-point scale is used with three possible responses: LOW, MEDIUM, and HIGH. A place is also included for a "not applicable" response.

After completing the job matrix, the participant was asked to rate his overall performance against his expectations during the last three months. This scale also includes ten possible response points with three points each for PARTIALLY ACHIEVING EXPECTATIONS, ACHIEVING EXPECTATIONS, and EX-

CEEDING EXPECTATIONS. A final response is available for individuals who felt the question was unacceptable.

8

Data Analysis

The limitations of a field study created a relatively small sample size of telecommuting and control individuals and lowered the researcher's control over the experimental environment. As a result, several techniques of analysis were necessary. These techniques included collecting and reporting subjective critical incidents expressed by telecommuters, descriptive graphical techniques, and statistical regressions techniques including an analysis of covariance.

This chapter presents a detailed coverage of each of these techniques and the manner in which they were used and interpreted. Each of the techniques possess advantages and disadvantages over the others but complimented each other when the results were integrated.

Three techniques of data analysis were used to interpret the results of the data obtained from this experimental design. Critical incidents were gathered to help interpret the outcomes obtained by graphical and statistical analysis. Descriptive graphical charts were used to visually examine the results. Statistical analysis was used to determine what outcomes bore a significant causal connection to the telecommuting treatment.

Critical Incidents

The most subjective data obtained from the study included a large number of so-called "critical incidents" of telecommuting. The use of critical incidents is generally accredited to the work of Flanagan[1] in 1954.

The technique basically consists of a series of procedures to log direct observations of human behavior from individuals which will be useful in solving and understanding practical problems and developing broad principles. This technique was used to gather important facts concerning behavioral effects of telecommuting. No single set of rigid rules was used; rather, some flexible principles established by Flanagan were modified and adapted to the specific situations involved with telecommuting.

An incident was defined as any "observable human activity that is sufficiently complete in itself to permit inferences and predictions to be made about the person performing the act."[2] The incident was "critical" if it occurred "in a situation where the purpose or the intent of the act seems fairly clear to the observer and where its consequences are sufficiently definite to leave little doubt concerning its effects."[3]

The use of the critical incident technique provided insight into the effects of telecommuting by presenting specific situations in which telecommuting had either benefited or impaired a particular class of outcomes such as communication. By integrating the objective questionnaire data with the subjective critical incident data, a better understanding of the forces at work on the organizational and behavioral outcomes imposed by telecommuting was gained.

Descriptive Graphical Techniques

A descriptive graphical technique was used to examine visually the effects of telecommuting upon the outcome variables. While the graphical presentation does not by itself provide statistical conclusion validity, it does indicate possible causal effects of telecommuting especially if supported by underlying critical incidents. A graphical effect which was unsupported by critical incidents was considered to result from measurement error or reliability and validity problems. The following discussion shows several possible graphical presentations.[4] The discussion also considers several possible erroneous interpretations of the graphs and the methods used to avoid them.

One possible graphical result of an outcome variable such as, "time spent communicating using the computer," given one pretreatment and one post-test measure, is shown on the following page. A "C" represents a control group mean while a "T" represents the mean obtained from the telecommuters. This graphical outcome could indicate that the group of telecommuters actually increased the amount of computer-based communication after beginning to work at home, and that this was due to telecommuting. However, several other possible effects could also be the cause.

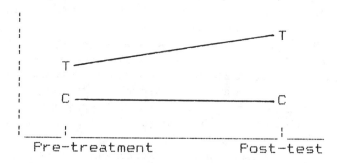

First, the possibility of selection-maturation, instead of telecommuting, could have produced this outcome. This could arise when one of the groups was growing faster than the other group because of selection differences. Observation and examination of the pretreatment environment along with critical incidents were used to determine the correct interpretation in such instances.

A second problem in the interpretation of this graphical outcome deals with instrumentation. Scaling problems in the questionnaire may have made it easier to detect changes at some points on the scale than at other points. Additionally, floor and ceiling problems may have occurred especially if the means approached either end of the scale. An inspection of the pretreatment and post-test frequency distributions was made to determine whether instrumentation problems were present. In some cases, it was possible to rescale the scores; in others, the problem persisted and resulted in a lack of interpretability.

A third problem that might have created the preceding outcome is differential statistical regression. This problem could result as a consequence of having a predetermined group of high scorers in the experimental group. The problem was avoided in this research since the the selection of control individuals was not based upon any pretreatment scores.

A fourth possible interpretation problem would result from an interaction of selection and history. Events other than the treatment which affected the experimental group but not the control group, or vice versa, may have produced the results. For example, the latter part of the experiment took place during the beginning of the winter months in Minnesota. Telecommuters were often able to stay at home and work while the control workers either could not work due to the weather or were adversely affected. This type of "local history" problem could have produced the results. The effect of weather in this example could be an effect of telecommuting that is of interest; however, knowing that it was the weather that produced the differential result, and not a direct attribute of telecommuting, is important to the correct interpretation of the outcome. Critical incidents were used in such instances to correctly interpret the possible effects of local history.

Another possible graphical outcome is illustrated below. This outcome indicates that both the telecommuting and control group are growing, but the rates of growth are different.

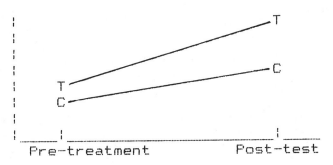

Cook and Campbell[5] note that it is common "to find differences in growth rates, particularly when respondents self-select themselves into receiving a treatment," as was the case in this research.

Self-selection resulted in the formation of a telecommuting group made up of individuals that were interested in telecommuting from their homes. It might be expected then that the telecommuting group would be more likely to experience higher rates of growth in some outcomes than would the control individuals. This problem was partially dealt with by the selection process used to obtain control subjects. However, it was impossible to completely control the self-selection problem, and this possible interpretation persisted.

A third possible graphical result has all of the aforementioned problems of interpretation, but in the opposite direction.

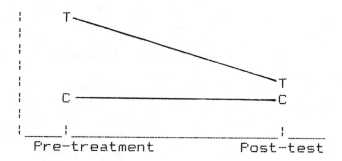

Such a result might be expected for questions such as "the amount of time spent communicating face-to-face." In this example the treatment group began with a much higher level of face-to-face communication. After beginning to telecommute, the treatment individuals experienced a much lower level of communication which approximately equaled that of the control group. As with the other possible outcomes, critical incidents were used to help in the correct interpretation of the outcome.

The final graphical outcome is the most interpretable result. In the cases of the previous graphs, there were no interaction patterns.

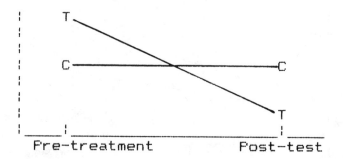

The intersection in this graph indicates that the two group means have switched. The high scoring group of telecommuters have fallen below the level of the control group.

The interacting graph is more easily interpreted since the problems mentioned are less likely to occur. The problem of selection-maturation is unlikely since "so few documented maturation patterns can be described in terms of trends that meet and cross over as opposed to trends that never meet and grow continuously further apart."[6] Scaling problems are unlikely since the interaction cannot be removed by transformation, and ceiling and floor problems cannot explain the crossover of the means. Regression towards the mean can also be discounted since there is no reason to suspect that a high treatment mean would regress to a lower grand mean.

Statistical Analysis Techniques

The statistical data analysis began by obtaining descriptive statistics for the outcome variables. The mean, variance, and standard deviation of the responses to each question on the questionnaires were obtained. Items which were additive such as the responses belonging to the same factor on the Minnesota Satisfaction Questionnaire were summed before computing these statistics.

After obtaining these initial statistics, the statistical analysis focused on using an analysis of covariance (ANCOVA) with a single covariate. This technique was deemed the most appropriate statistical procedure for analyzing data gathered by the research. The heavy reliance upon the ANCOVA to statistically analyze the data requires a brief discussion of this technique as it was used in the research.

The ANCOVA technique is an extension of the elementary analysis of variance (ANOVA) technique. The ANOVA model computes the grand mean of the post-test scores across all individuals in the sample. This grand mean is the average response on the measurement scale used in the question being analyzed. The ANOVA model then computes the treatment effect which is the averaged amount that the treatment, telecommuting, adds to or subtracts from the post-test scores in the telecommuting group. Finally, the residual effect or error is computed. This error is representative of the effects of all factors other than telecommuting which have contributed to the differences between the scores of the telecommuting group and the control group. Error is a result of unreliable measurement and reliable individual differences between the two groups. The ANOVA model is constructed upon the assumption that the error or residual effect is normally and independently distributed with a mean of zero and a constant variance.

The ANOVA unlike the ANCOVA model would not use the pre-telecommuting scores in its analysis. Information concerning the initial group differences obtained from the pretelecommuting scores are ignored and included in the residual effect. The ANCOVA model extends the ANOVA model to incorporate this additional pretelecommuting information in the form of a linear regression.[7]

Using this additional information created a more powerful test of the telecommuting effect. However, this adjustment of the telecommuting effect by the pretelecommuting information alters the expected value of the telecommuting effect estimate. The ANCOVA model was used to determine if the telecommuting groups scored higher or lower on a particular outcome variable by a greater degree than would be expected given the initial selection differences found in the pretelecommuting measure of the same outcome variable.

> Thus the estimate of the treatment effect in the ANCOVA is the difference between the predicted post-test scores of individuals in the two groups who have been "matched" on pretest scores. A statistically significant difference then "suggests" that one group would have significantly outperformed the other on the post-test *if the groups had started with the same pretest scores.*[8]

The extension of the experimental model described by Cook and Campbell to include two post-test measures also extended the form of the ANCOVA model utilized. The statistical design was a repeated-measures ANCOVA model using one grouping variable, one trial variable, and one covariate that is constant over trials.[9] The two post-test measures constituted the repeated measures; the grouping variable indicated whether the individual was in the telecommuting or control group; the trial variable was the responses to a particular question; and the covariate was the pretelecommuting measure of the corresponding question.

The repeated measures ANCOVA model provided mean square estimates and F-scores for the effects of telecommuting, the pretelecommuting score, the effect of time on the post-test scores, the interaction between time and group, and the residual error.

The ability of the research to utilize the statistical results found by the ANCOVA model to "suggest" the possibility of a significant connection between telecommuting and the observed outcomes variables was limited by a variety of influences.

First, the small sample size was a continuing problem. The power of the ANCOVA model to detect group differences varied, depending upon the mean square error which was occasionally quite large. That is, the ability of the ANCOVA technique to detect a difference in the group means was often quite weak. In these instances, only a very large telecommuting effect would have been detectable; therefore, moderate effects imposed by telecommuting on some outcome variables may have been unnoticed by the ANCOVA model. To partially overcome this problem, "possible" causal connections are reported in the next chapter that were supported by critical incidents and graphical results, but which failed to produce statistically significant results. Such reports of cause can only be used as possible influences of telecommuting to be tested in future research.

The small sample size also created other problems. Like the ANOVA model, the ANCOVA model assumes a normal independently distributed set of residuals with a mean of zero and constant variance. In the repeated measures design used in the experiment (i.e., two post-test measures), the F-tests were made "in a way that allows some relaxation of the assumption of complete independence."[10] The testing of the other assumptions of the residual terms was unavailable to the researcher; however, it must be assumed that violations were likely. Therefore, even statistically significant results must be examined with an understanding that possible assumptions may have been violated. Again, support from both graphs and critical incidents played an important role in strengthening the validity of the reported findings.

Other problems stemming from the implementation of the experimental design may have affected the estimate of the telecommuting effect. Possible bias may have been introduced into the ANCOVA procedure by the quality of the measuring instruments and by changing the questions from the pretelecommuting to the post-test periods. Cook and Campbell[11] point out that sources of bias can result from the ANCOVA model adjusting the treatment effect by the group pretelecommuting differences. Random measurement error, especially with the small sample size used in this research, not only can reduce the precision of the statistical procedure, but can introduce biased treatment effects. "Measurement error in the pretreatment responses can therefore produce spurious treatment effects when none exist."[12]

Several other kinds of bias were likely to occur in the experiment. One possible source of bias arose from the use of various organizations and jobs within each of the groups creating subpopulations which may have grown at different rates. Since ANCOVA uses the within-group growth patterns to estimate the between-group growth patterns, bias may have been introduced. Other sources of bias in the estimated effect of telecommuting may be due to components in the pretelecommuting measures which are unrelated to both the post-test scores and selection differences and the complex structure and nature of human behavior. Additionally, since the ANCOVA model used a linear regression technique to account for the pretelecommuting information, nonlinear regression lines and nonparallel regression lines can create spurious results and interpretation problems.

A final concern in interpreting the statistical results produced from the ANCOVA technique stems from the large number of outcome variables measured and tested. The likelihood of falsely concluding that a relationship existed between telecommuting and a particular outcome variable increases when multiple comparisons of many outcome variables are made. Recognition was given to the fact that a certain proportion of the comparisons would be significantly different by chance alone. Again, the use of critical incidents was relied upon to dissociate the effects which might have resulted only by chance from those which had underlying behavioral reasons for their occurrence.

9

Research Results

This chapter presents the important statistical and graphical results of the differences in organizational and behavioral outcome variables among the telecommuting and control groups. These group differences were investigated using statistical and graphical analysis of objective questionnaire data. The next chapter uses subjective observations and critical incidents to summarize and interpret the findings presented in this chapter and suggests possible causal links between telecommuting and the outcome variables.

It became obvious during the course of the experiment and during the analysis of the data that the experiences of the telecommuting group largely depended upon the number of days per week that a participant spent working at home.

Of the sixteen telecommuters, twelve participants were able to successfully telecommute from their homes. Six participants successfully adopted telecommuting on a full-time basis working at home four to five days per week. The other six telecommuters adopted telecommuting on a part-time basis working at home two to three days per week. The remaining four telecommuters worked at home only occasionally (less than two days per week). These four individuals were unable to work actively at home and their experience with telecommuting was considered unsuccessful. Table 1 illustrates the correspondence between the number of days the telecommuters worked at home, their organizations, and their jobs.

Table 1.   Comparison of the Extent of
Telecommuting with Organizations and Jobs

Extent of Telecommuting	Organization	Job
Full-time (4-5 Days/Week)	Company 1	Word Processing
	Company 3	Programmer
	Company 4	Programmer
	Company 5	Programmer
Part-time (2-3 Days/Week)	Company 2	Program Developer
		Designer
Unable (2 Days/Week)	Company 2	Editor
		Text Developer

The extent to which participants were able to telecommute on a full-time or part-time basis was determined by the participating organization. The employees who worked at home part-time did not have the option of extending their telecommuting days to full-time; however, they could reduce their telecommuting days if they felt that telecommuting was not possible or detrimental to their jobs. The individuals who were unable to telecommute successfully took this option. The full-time employees did not have the option of working at home part-time.

The number of days that a telecommuter worked at home was an extremely important determinant in the organizational and behavioral effects of telecommuting. In general, when this difference was not considered in the analysis, no effects of telecommuting were found. However, when the telecommuting participants were grouped according to the number of days they worked at home several important differences emerged. Unfortunately, this grouping also created sample size problems since separation of the treatment group into the three categories (full-time, part-time, and unable) strained the already low degrees of freedom. Only those results which were additionally supported by observations and critical incidents were considered valid; but, caution in interpretation must be observed.

Important Findings

Because of the large number of outcome variables only the important research findings are presented. Results were considered important if they demonstrated statistical or graphical differences between either the control and telecommuting groups or among the control, full-time, part-time, and unable groups. Appendix B contains some of the detailed statistical and graphical findings which support these results.

Demographic Differences

Several demographic variables were obtained from the participants during the pretreatment time period. Tables B.1 and B.2 in Appendix B present the descriptive statistics and ANOVA comparisons of these variables which concerned:

- Age
- Sex
- Number of years in the organization
- Number of years in their current position
- Education
- Number of other individuals living with the participant
- Age of children in the household
- Commuting distance to work

No differences between the control and telecommuting group were found due to the matching process used to select the control participants. Additionally, no differences in the demographic variables among the control, full-time, part-time, and unable groups were found except for the number of other individuals living at home with the telecommuting participants. The full-time telecommuting group had larger households (more children) than the other groups.

While other statistical differences in the demographic variables were not found, two observations should be noted. First, all but one of the full-time telecommuters were female, while the part-time telecommuters were largely male. Second, the full-time group had a large variance in education and time in the organization and job position since the word processing telecommuters were newly hired and had less education than the other participants.

Communication Differences

Hypotheses H1 through H3 stated that telecommuting was expected to decrease horizontal, upward, and downward communication. Tables B.3. and B.4 in Appendix B present the descriptive statistics and ANCOVA results concerning these communication questions. Figures B.1 through B.4 show the graphical analysis of the communication questions.

Several differences in communication were found among the control, full-time, part-time, and unable groups.

Evidence concerning full-time telecommuters indicated that:

- Face-to face communication decreased and was much lower than that of the other groups.
- Horizontal communication concerning job related subjects decreased.
- Upward communication decreased and was lower than that of the other groups.
- Subordinate communication decreased and was lower than that of the other groups.

Evidence concerning part-time telecommuters indicated that:

- Horizontal communication did not decrease due to an increase in telephone and computer communications.
- Upward communication with supervisors increased resulting in a level that was higher than that of the other groups. However, a time-group interaction indicated that this increase in upward communication may not be sustained.
- Subordinate communication levels increased and were higher than those of the other groups. Telephone and computer communication was often used

to communicate with subordinates and appeared to moderate any loss in their subordinate communication.

Table 2 summarizes the changes in communication variables.

Table 2. Summary of Changes in Communication Outcomes

Communication Variable	Full-Time Telecommuters	Part-Time Telecommuters	Unable Telecommuters
Face-to-Face	Decrease	Increase	Increase
Horizontal	Decrease	Increase	None
Upward	Decrease	Increase	None
Downward	Decrease	Increase	Increase

Full-time telecommuters experienced a substantial drop in all levels of communication. Conversely, the group of telecommuters who were unable to work actively at home indicated a large increase in face-to-face communication that appeared to be partly responsible for their inability to work at home. Part-time telecommuters experienced moderate increases in all types of communication.

Evidence to support hypotheses H1, H2, and H3 concerning a reduction in communication as a result of telecommuting existed for the participants who worked at home full-time. Further discussion of these results and possible interpretations are presented in the next chapter.

Spatial-Physical Differences

Hypothesis H4 stated that telecommuting would increase spatial-physical barriers thereby reducing the telecommuter's ability to ask questions, talk with people, and access needed resource materials. Tables B.5 and B.6 and figures B.5 through B.7 in Appendix B present the descriptive statistics, ANCOVA results, and graphical analysis of these spatial-physical questions.

Some differences in the effects of spatial-physical distances among the control, full-time, part-time, and unable groups were indicated.

Full-time telecommuters experienced a large decrease in the time spent with their work group. This finding supports hypothesis H4. The amount of time a question was not asked because of physical separation was also high for the full-time telecommuting group during the first three months of the experiment. During the second three months of the experiment, they reported lower responses indicating a time effect. This time effect was due to the initial remote job training of the newly hired word processing operators.

The telecommuters who were unable to work actively at home spent much more time with their work group and this was one of the reasons they were unable to work at home according to schedule. Additionally, the unable group reported a reduction in access to needed reference materials when they worked at home.

The successful part-time participants needed fewer reference materials than those in the unable group. For example, the programming participants had many of their needed resources on-line to their home computer or terminal. However, the part-time participants reported that a concentrated effort was necessary to make sure that they took home any resources and materials needed to work at home.

Table 3 summarizes the changes in spatial-physical distance variables.

Table 3.
Changes in Spatial-Physical Distance Outcomes

Spatial-Physical Variables	Full-Time Group	Part-Time Group	Unable Group
Time Away from Work Group	Increase	Decrease	Decrease
Face-to-Face Communication Impossible	Increase	Decrease	Decrease
Questions Could not be Asked	None	None	None
Times when no one to Talk with	None	None	None
Unavailable References and Resources	None	None	Increase

Job Task Differences

Hypotheses H6 through H8 concerned the job task outcomes. Tables B.5 and B.6 and figure B.8 in Appendix B present the descriptive statistics, ANCOVA results, and graphical analysis of questions concerning the interdependence and complexity of job tasks.

Telecommuting decreased the amount of time a job was dependent upon other team members for those telecommuters who initially had high levels of job interdependence. Full-time telecommuters also indicated a higher inability to work due to equipment failure during the first three months. Both of these findings support hypothesis H6.

The full-time telecommuting group experienced a decrease in their job tasks. Full-time word processing telecommuters had their jobs limited only to tasks concerning the reception, transcribing, and transmission of documents to be typed. The word processing workers in the control group also typed from hard copy, supervised the tasks of new workers, and printed documents. Full-time programmers were unable to help in the job training and supervision of new workers, and their programming tasks involved less coordination with subordinates, users, and team members. These findings support hypothesis H7 which stated that telecommuting was expected to reduce the number of job tasks a worker was expected to perform.

Hypothesis H8 stated that telecommuting was expected to make the telecommuter's job more uncertain or ill-structured. No indication that participation in the telecommuting experiment affected task uncertainty was found.

Table 4 summarizes the job task changes that were observed during the telecommuting experiment.

Table 4. Changes in Job Task Outcomes

Job Task Outcome	Full-Time Group	Part-Time Group	Unable Group
Interdependence	None	Decrease	Decrease
Number of Tasks	Decrease	None	None
Complexity	None	None	None

Organizational Behavior Differences

Hypothesis H9 through H11 considered the effects of telecommuting upon individual, intragroup, and vertical organizational behavior. Tables B.7 and B.8 and Figures B.9 through B.13 in Appendix B present the descriptive statistics, ANCOVA results, and graphical analysis of the organizational behavior questions.

No differences among the groups concerning individual organizational behavior were found during the telecommuting experiment. However, some time effects were observed between the three and six month time periods. During the second three months of the telecommuting experiment:

- Full-time telecommuters experienced a decrease in the extent to which work breaks were automatically shortened when work needed to be done.
- All telecommuters experienced a decrease in their extent of trying to improve work methods to solve work problems, while the control participants experienced an increase.
- Part-time and full-time telecommuters experienced a drop in their contentment with the job.
- Part-time telecommuters experienced a decline in their sense of achievement in performing the job.

Hypothesis H9 stated that telecommuting would adversely affect a telecommuter's individual organizational behavior. While no differences among the groups were obtained to support hypothesis H9, it would appear that some deterioration in individual organizational behavior occurred during the second three months of the experiment. If this trend continued, differences would be expected to emerge.

Hypothesis H10 stated that telecommuting would adversely affect intragroup organizational behavior. Part-time telecommuters experienced a decrease in identification with their work group which supports this hypothesis.

Support for hypothesis H11 which indicated that telecommuting would adversely affect vertical organizational behavior was not found. Some subjective evidence suggested that vertical relations for some of the telecommuters actually improved.

Table 5 summarizes the findings concerning organizational behavior.

Table 5.
Changes in Organizational Behavioral Outcomes

Org. Behavior Outcome	Full-Time Group	Part-Time Group	Unable Group
Individual	Decrease*	Decrease*	None
Intragroup	None	Decrease	None
Vertical	None	None	None

* = time effect

Job Satisfaction Differences

Telecommuting was expected to decrease a telecommuter's job satisfaction according to hypothesis H13. Tables B.9 and B.10 and figure B.14 in Appendix B present the descriptive statistics, ANCOVA results, and graphical analysis of the twenty job satisfaction dimensions measured by the Minnesota Satisfaction Questionnaire.

Analysis of the questionnaire data found several differences among the control, full-time, part-time, and unable groups concerning job satisfaction.

- All telecommuters reported lower levels of satisfaction concerning office working conditions, while the control group reported no change.
- Part-time telecommuters reported higher satisfaction concerning their ability to work alone, while the full-time telecommuters reported lower satisfaction.
- Full-time telecommuters reported lower satisfaction concerning the amount of variety in their jobs.
- Part-time telecommuters reported lower satisfaction concerning their ability to direct the actions of others.
- Full-time telecommuters reported lower satisfaction concerning job security.

These findings were additionally supported by the observations that:

- Full-time telecommuters generally had children at home which restricted their ability to work alone. Part-time telecommuters generally did not have children at home.
- Full-time telecommuters performed a restricted subset of the job tasks normally performed by their peers. The job tasks of part-time telecommuters remained largely unchanged.
- Part-time telecommuters reported that they would be unable to take on additional responsibilities which would require the supervision of subordinates.
- The word processing telecommuters were aware that they were participating in an experimental program which if terminated would cost them their jobs.

The Minnesota Satisfaction Questionnaire data also indicated several time effects which occurred between the three and six month experimental periods. However, most of these time effects followed a pattern in which the telecommuters rated the dimension higher in the first experimental period, but lower in the second experimental period. The decline in the second experimental period did not produce a satisfaction level which was lower than their pretelecommuting response. It was likely that these time effects can be explained as a Hawthorne phenomenon which produced abnormally high responses during the first period and regression towards the mean during the second.

However, two time effects cannot be dismissed as Hawthorne effects. First, satisfaction with office working conditions continued to deteriorate during the second half of the experiment. Second, part-time telecommuters experienced a decline in their satisfaction concerning opportunities for job advancement during the six month period which was below that indicated during either of the previous two periods. Observation and critical incidents indicated that part-time telecommuters felt that working at home would not hurt their advancement opportunities during the pretelecommuting period and the first three months of the experiment. During the second three months of the experiment, part-time telecommuters became cognizant of the negative effect that telecommuting was having upon their opportunities for advancement.

Table 6 summarizes the changes in job satisfaction outcomes.

Attitude Differences

Hypotheses H14 through H16 concerned the effect of telecommuting upon the at-

Table 6.
Summary of Changes in Job Satisfaction Outcomes

Job Satisfaction Dimension	Full-Time Group	Part-Time Group	Unable Group
Ability to Work Alone on the Job	Decrease	Increase	Increase
Amount of Variety on the Job	Decrease	Same	Increase
Ability to Direct Actions to Others	Same	Decrease	Increase
Job Security	Decrease	Increase	Increase
Office Working Conditions	Decrease	Decrease*	Decrease
Opportunities for Advancement	Decrease	Decrease*	Increase

* = time effect

titude towards working at home of the telecommuters, their managers, and their co-workers. No support for these hypotheses was found.

Performance Differences

Productivity for both telecommuting and control groups was rated better than average by managers and participants prior to beginning the telecommuting experiment. Generally, the productivity of the telecommuters was slightly higher than the control participants but this difference was not significant. No evidence to support hypothesis H12 which stated that telecommuting would adversely affect performance, turnover, and absenteeism was found. Some subjective evidence existed to indicate that performance actually improved for some of the members of the telecommuting group.

Hypothesis H5 stated that performance measurement and monitoring would decrease as a result of telecommuting. Performance measurement and monitoring of the full-time word processing telecommuters was on an hourly basis which was much more frequent than the daily monitoring of the control individuals in the central word processing pool. Full-time programmers and the part-time telecommuters made weekly written progress reports to their managers. In only one case did the manager of a control individual require this close of supervision over performance. This evidence is contrary to hypothesis H5. Performance measurement and monitoring actually increased for the telecommuters.

Effect of Technology

The objective of hypotheses H17 through H25 was to determine the ability of technology to moderate the negative effects of telecommuting from the home. Tables B.11 and B.12 and figures B.15 through B.20 in Appendix B present the descriptive statistics, ANCOVA results, and graphical analysis of telephone and computer usage. The moderation effect of using technology on the outcome variables was investigated by:

1. Examining the changes in the use of telecommunications and computer technology which could be attributed to telecommuting.
2. Comparing these changes in technology usage with the changes (or lack of changes) in the outcome variables. Observations and critical incidents were used to determine the extent to which the change in technology usage moderated the changes in the outcome variables.

A summary of the findings in step 1 indicates that:

- Use of the telephone for communication increased as a result of telecommuting. The extent of the increase depended upon the number of days the telecommuter worked at home.
- Use of the computer for communication with group members, supervisors, and users did not increase as a result of telecommuting.
- Use of the computer for subordinate communication increased for the part-time and full-time groups.
- The extent to which a job was dependent upon the computer and telephone increased as a result of telecommuting.
- The increased use of the computer for communicating with other group members and users for the group which was unable to work actively at home was due to the introduction of office word processors, not the use of home computers or terminals. The unable group also found the office word processors, not home computers or terminals, important to their jobs.

Support for hypothesis H17 which stated that the use of technology would moderate the extent that communication was affected by telecommuting was observed. Telephone communications appeared to be effective for the majority of communications when conversations tended to be informational in nature (getting the answer to some question), providing progress status, and giving task instructions. However, some types of conversations were not conducive to the phone media. Conversations concerning performance review, either with managers or subordinates, initial project design conversations with clients or project members, and final reviews for evaluation and revision, were seen as unacceptable via the phone.

These types of communication required face-to-face forums so that the reactions of the receiver could be judged, and statements or discussions tempered by those observations.

Part-time telecommuters did not experience a noticeable drop in communication since the proportion of communication which could be handled by phone and the proportion of communication which required face-to-face contact matched the extent of their telecommuting. Since part-time telecommuters generally spent two days per week in the office, they arranged their communication needs to coincide with their location. However, it was apparent that without the phone, communication would have decreased for these workers.

Full-time telecommuters did experience a noticeable drop in communication. Their needs for face-to-face communication were greater than their full-time telecommuting status could accommodate. Additionally, while telephone communication increased, this channel lacked sufficient breadth to substitute for all of their communication needs. While it was evident that the telephone moderated their decrease in communication, the technology was unable to fully substitute for all communications.

The use of telephone and computer technologies helped to increase performance measurement and monitoring for the word processing telecommuters. For example, the office manager was able to determine the extent to which a telecommuting word processing employee was working by observing the turnaround (or lack thereof) of documents sent to the worker's home. Without the use of telecommunications to transmit the finished documents, the turnaround would have been daily at a minimum and probably much longer. However, telephone and computer technologies did not play a significant role in the performance measurement and monitoring of the other telecommuters. Therefore, only limited support for hypothesis H18 which concerned the ability of telephone and computer technology to moderate a decrease in performance measurement and monitoring was found.

Evidence was reported to indicate that the decline in job interdependence of the telecommuters would have been more significant without the use of telecommunication and computer technologies. Part-time telecommuters were able to remain active on project teams, and they continued to supervise subordinates by increasing their use of telephone and computer technology. Word processing telecommuters found that the final stage of the transcription task, printing, was performed by someone else. In emergencies, they also found that dictation could be routed to other word processing telecommuters giving them the feeling that they were in fact working within a work group. Full-time programmers would have found their jobs less dependent upon others if telecommunications and computer technology had not increased. This evidence supports hypothesis H19 and suggested that telecommunications and computer technology did play a moderating role in what could have been a much larger decline in job interdependence.

Hypothesis H20 addressed the ability of telecommunications and computer technology to moderate changes in job tasks which were expected to occur as a result of telecommuting. Evidence indicated that without the use of technology, the word processing and programming jobs could not have been involved in telecommuting. Likewise, the jobs of part-time telecommuters would have changed to a degree that would have been unacceptable to the workers if technology usage had not increased. These observations support hypothesis H20.

Hypothesis H21 concerned the ability of technology to moderate an increase in complexity (ill-structuredness) of job tasks that was expected to result from telecommuting. The only indication of an increase in job complexity occurred for the word processing telecommuters during the initial weeks of working at home. Since they were new to the organization and two of the three had never worked on a word processor, job complexity was high during this training period. The telephone was used extensively to reduce the ill-structuredness associated with this period, and it is doubtful whether these telecommuters would have become productive without using the telephone. Also, some of the full-time programmers and part-time telecommuters reported using both the telephone and computer communications to ask questions and clarify their job tasks with others in their project groups. These limited observations indicated that the telephone was used to reduce the complexity or ill-structuredness of a job, especially for initial job training.

Hypotheses H22 through H24 concerned the ability of telecommunications and computer technology to moderate a decrease in attitude towards working at home that was expected to result from telecommuting. Telecommuters found that by using the telephone and computer for communications they could remain in touch with the organization and co-workers. The feeling that isolation from the organization would result from telecommuting was the most important negative belief concerning the attitude of telecommuters, their managers, and their co-workers about working at home. Generally, the use of technology helped alleviate this fear and thereby allowed attitudes to remain positive.

Hypothesis H25 concerned the ability of technology to moderate a decrease in job satisfaction that was expected to occur as a result of telecommuting. No direct link between using technology and job satisfaction was observed except for those that have already been mentioned. Using technology moderated the loss in communications and prevented many job task changes that would otherwise have been necessary. Therefore using telecommunications and computer technology indirectly moderated a loss in job satisfaction.

In summary, observation and critical incidents indicated that the use of technology played an important role in moderating the negative influences of working at home on the outcome variables. Table 7 summarizes the findings concerning the moderating role of technology.

Table 7. Evidence that Using Technology
Moderated the Effects of Telecommuting

Outcome Moderated By Technology	Full-Time Group	Part-Time Group	Unable Group
Extent of Commun- ication	Yes	Yes	No
Performance Measurement and Monitoring	Yes	No	No
Job Interdependence	Yes	Yes	No
Job Tasks	Yes	Yes	No
Job Complexity	Yes	Yes	No
Attitude Towards Working at Home	Yes	Yes	No
Job Satisfaction	Indirect	Indirect	No

Summary of Results

The effects of telecommuting upon the various outcome variables associated with the hypotheses were investigated by combining evidence obtained from:

1. Descriptive and ANCOVA statistics of questionnaire answers.
2. Graphical analysis of the trend of questionnaire responses.
3. Observation and critical incidents obtained during the interviews.

The hypotheses were not accepted or rejected in a classical sense. Rather, support or lack of support for a hypothesis was examined and these findings are summarized in table 8.

It is difficult to draw general conclusions of the organizational and behavioral effects of telecommuting from only the findings presented in this chapter. Conclusions must be examined within the multitude of confounding influences and events which occurred within the organizations and individuals during the course of the telecommuting experiment. In the next chapter, observations and critical incidents are used to explain these findings by developing scenarios of the telecommuting experiences for the three groups of telecommuters. These scenarios provide the backdrop against which the findings reported in this chapter can be melded to form a coherent picture of the organizational and behavioral effects of telecommuting.

Table 8.
Summary of Evidence concerning
the Hypotheses Investigated

Hypothesis	Full-Time Group	Part-Time Group	Unable Group
Communication:			
H1-Horizontal	Yes	No	No
H2-Upward	Yes	No	No
H3-Vertical	Yes	No	No
Spatial-Physical:			
H4-Outcomes	Some	No	No
Job Tasks:			
H6-Interdependence	No	Yes	Yes
H7-Number of Tasks	Yes	No	No
H8-Complexity	No	No	No
Organizational Behavior:			
H9-Individual	Some*	Some*	No
H10-Intragroup	No	Some	No
H11-Vertical	No	No	No
Job Satisfaction:			
H13-Outcomes	Some	Some	No
Attitude:			
H14-Telecommuter	No	No	No
H15-Manager	No	No	No
H16-Co-worker	No	No	No
Performance:			
H12-Performance	No	No	No
H5-Monitoring	No	No	No
Technology Moderation:			
H17-Communication	Yes	Yes	No
H18-Monitoring	Yes	No	No
H19-Interdependence	Yes	Yes	No
H20-Job Tasks	Yes	Yes	No
H21-Job Complexity	Yes	Yes	No
H22-H24-Attitude	Yes	Yes	No
H25-Job Satisfaction	Some	Some	No

* = time effect

10

Scenarios

Scenarios of the findings for the full-time and part-time telecommuters, along with the group of telecommuters who are unable to work actively at home are used to summarize the results of this research. A scenario is constructed by combining the results of the various organizational and behavioral variables with the observations and critical incidents that are obtained from the interviews. This approach places the results in the organizational and behavioral context in which they occurred and allows generalizations and interpretations to be made within that context.

Separate scenarios are developed for the full-time and part-time telecommuters and the group that is unable to work actively at home because of the important differences in their telecommuting experiences. A separate scenario for the group of telecommuters who are unable to work at home is developed to help understand the problems which prevented them from actively working at home.

Full-time Telecommuters

Full-time telecommuters differ from the other groups of telecommuters, not only in certain demographic and personal characteristics, but most importantly in their experiences with telecommuting. The interaction between their demographic and personal situations and their experiences with telecommuting provides the necessary context from which generalizations and interpretations can be made. This interaction is discussed first by examining the demographic and personal characteristics of the full-time telecommuters and then relating these to the effects of telecommuting.

Demographic and Personal Characteristics

Full-time telecommuters worked at home more than four days per week during the experiment. They are from four different organizations. Three full-time telecommuters are from Company 1 and work as word processing employees. The other three full-time telecommuters come from three different organizations, Companies 3, 4, and 5, and are all computer programmers. All of the full-time telecommuters, except for the programmer from Company 5, are women with preschool children at home. The programmer from Company 5 is atypical of this group since he is a bachelor who works at home because of a shortage of office space. During the fifth month of the experimental period, new office space was constructed, and this telecommuter returned to the office to work.

Of the three word processing employees in Company 1, two quit work to stay home and raise their children while the third quit a word processing job at another organization to participate in the telecommuting experiment. All three have a very strong desire to stay home and raise their children. Working at home is desirable since it satisfies certain financial needs and also enables these individuals to be at home and raise their children.

Of the two computer programmers who have children at home, one was planning to quit her job in order to stay home and raise her children. This participant's organization decided to experiment with telecommuting as a means of retaining a valuable employee and at the same time accommodating her needs to personally rear her children. The other computer programmer with children at home was faced with child care costs which would make work unprofitable during the summer months. This participant's organization decided to experiment with telecommuting to ease her financial child care burden. After the summer was over, this telecommuter somewhat reluctantly returned to work at the office. Her reluctance was due to a desire to experience working at home while the school age children were away at school to determine if telecommuting would be easier and more productive in a quieter home.

Aside from providing these telecommuters with the ability to stay home and raise their children, the participating organizations also hope to gain information which would be useful in evaluating the future of telecommuting in their organization. The organizations see telecommuting as a promising work alternative which can be used to attract and retain employees. Also, Company 5, views telecommuting as a possible means to overcome an office space shortage which might alleviate future office expansion needs.

Telecommuting Experiences

Full-time telecommuters experience a drop in communication — especially face-to-face communication — and an increase in the time spent away from their work groups. Almost all communication while at home is by telephone.

Critical incidents reveal that the nature of this phone communication is almost totally work related, informational in character, and of immediate importance to accomplishing the current task.

"If I have a problem or question, I'll call up _____ or the author and get an answer."

Full-time telecommuters discard any communication needs that are not of this type. This is accomplished by making an appropriate assumption or leaving the final correction or coordination to someone else.

"Sometimes I'm not sure that the letter is in the right form, but _____ can fix it if its wrong."

Downward communication with subordinates is also affected by full-time telecommuting and indicates that full-time telecommuters have a difficult time communicating with subordinates.

"It would have been too difficult to supervise someone, so I gave up those responsibilities."

For full-time telecommuters, telephone and telecommunications technology are inadequate for directing subordinates and evaluating their performance.

Importantly, full-time telecommuters do not report that telecommuting affects the times in which questions cannot be asked, the times when no one is around to talk with, and the times when references and resources are unavailable. The lack of telecommuting effects upon these outcomes is due to the use of telecommunication and computer technology. The telephone is an adequate media for asking questions and talking with others.

"If someone isn't around to answer the phone, they wouldn't have been available to talk to in the office, either."

Also, the computers and word processors effectively provide the resources and references that are needed to perform the full-time telecommuters' jobs.

Full-time telecommuters experience changes in their job tasks. In all cases, the tasks that are performed by the full-time telecommuters are more restricted and specialized than those that are performed by their counterparts in the office. Tasks which require a design emphasis as opposed to a development emphasis are omitted. Certain tasks such as document printing for the word processing workers are omitted as a result of the technical systems configuration. Most importantly, tasks such as training new workers and building *esprit de corps* are impossible for the full-time telecommuters. While telecommunication and computer technology allows most of the full-time telecommuter's job to be performed at home, it is unable to prevent a loss of certain types of tasks.

Full-time telecommuters report that some behavioral outcomes that are associated with shortening work breaks if needed, and improving work methods deteriorate.

"How do I feel work pressures at home? I don't know when people are in a tizzy trying to get a project finished, I just work by my work plan and objectives."

Job contentment also shows some deterioration during the course of the experiment. This deterioration for one of the programmers is due to the loss of social contact with the organization and work group.

> "I miss the other people; I liked the social relationships at work and I would not want to do this telecommuting indefinitely."

The loss of job contentment for the other full-time telecommuters is often not directly attributed to telecommuting.

> "This [telecommuting] is wonderful! I am doing all the things [working and caring for my children] I want and I feel more fulfilled than I ever have."

However, this same telecommuter expresses concern about the job later in the same interview:

> ". . . the job isn't as good as I had. I was supervising several people and I liked that job better."

These problems are also reflected in a drop in satisfaction with the amount of variety in the job.

Managerial relations are also affected by telecommuting. The full-time telecommuters indicate that it is impractical to keep their managers constantly informed since they are seldom in the office. They rely upon work results instead of communication to demonstrate their performance and are resigned to the fact that managerial communication has decreased. As a result, they report a decline in their satisfaction with their opportunities for advancement.

Other declines in job satisfaction are reported by the full-time telecommuters concerning office working conditions and their ability to work alone on the job. Since all but one of the full-time telecommuters have small children who demand their attention, even during working hours, the decline in the telecommuters' satisfaction with their ability to work alone on the job is expected. Also, working at home and caring for children increases the level of stress that is associated with the job.

Despite these apparent declines in some aspects of the behavioral and satisfaction outcomes, most of the full-time telecommuters enjoy working at home. They have a good attitude which relates primarily to their feelings that they are able to work while at the same time care for their children. Their performance remains high throughout the experiment.

In summary, the jobs of the full-time telecommuters are not as enriched as those of their counterparts in the office. The use of technology is unable to prevent some loss in communication and the time spent away from their work group. These outcomes in turn necessitate assigning the full-time telecommuters a restricted set of job tasks and produces some loss in their job commitment, contentment, and satisfaction.

Those telecommuters who have strong personal reasons for wanting to work at home coupled with rational monetary reasons for wanting to work, experience the greatest success with telecommuting. That is, the telecommuters who feel they have to stay home and care for their children and who are primarily interested in only the monetary rewards of the job are better adjusted to full-time telecommuting than those who do not have a strong personal motivation to work at home or who are seeking self-actualizing or social needs from the job.

Part-time Telecommuters

Part-time telecommuters are those telecommuters who work at home four, or fewer, days per week. On the average they spend slightly less than three days per week working from their homes. Two of the part-time telecommuters work at home two days per week, one works at home four days per week, and the other three work at home three days per week. The part-time telecommuters differ from the full-time telecommuters in both demographic and personal characteristics and in their experiences with telecommuting.

Demographic and Personal Characteristics

All of the part-time telecommuters are from a single organization, Company 2, which is participating in a widespread experiment with telecommuting. Compared to the other organizations, Company 2 has the greatest experience with telecommuting and chose to allow their employees to telecommute part-time rather than full-time. All of the part-time telecommuters are either program designers or programming developers. While all but one of the full-time telecommuters have small children at home, only one of the part-time telecommuters has a child at home. Four of the part-time telecommuters are male while two are female.

The reasons that the part-time telecommuters want to work at home differ from those of the full-time telecommuters. Instead of having small children at home that need care, the homes of the part-time telecommuters are quiet, comfortable places to work. Their homes provide a place in which the part-time telecommuters can escape the interruptions of the office to work on mentally intensive writing, programming, and planning tasks. As such, work is organized and planned according to whether the telecommuter is going to be in the office or the home. Their motivation to work at home is based on their beliefs that working at home will increase their productivity and provide a more comfortable working environment.

Three of the part-time telecommuters are program designers. They are responsible for determining the feasibility of a project and designing and coordinating the development team effort. They also assure the quality of the finished product. As such, their jobs are largely divided into those tasks which require extensive face-to-face meetings and contacts with users and team members, and concentrated efforts in writing budgets, plans, need assessments, design specifications, and project documentation. The divisions in their job tasks match the days spent in the office and those spent in the home.

The other three part-time telecommuters are programming developers. Their tasks include developing computer programs that are used in projects. They make extensive use of computer and telecommunications technology in their homes. Except for meetings to coordinate team efforts, their jobs require little face-to-face contact.

Telecommuting Experiences

Unlike the full-time telecommuters, part-time telecommuters report very few effects of telecommuting. Telecommunications and computer technology play an important role in moderating the negative influences of telecommuting. Working at home has no detrimental effect on communication.

> "No, I never have problems getting my questions answered [at home]. I simply pick up the phone and call whoever I need. Actually, it's easier using the phone because I used to feel that I needed to see the person in person and would hang around his office. Now I don't waste my time; if he's not in, I leave a message."

Whereas the full-time telecommuter discards communication that is not work related, informational, and immediately important to the current task, it is simply deferred by the part-time telecommuters until they are in the office. As a result, they do not report a drop in the levels of their communication. However, devoting more office time to communicating instead of writing, programming, etc. causes some problems. Concern is expressed by several co-workers that this shift in tasks by part-time telecommuters is not productive.

> "When in the office, you can often see _____ holding court in the halls. Since _____ is doing work at home, the office has become a social interaction time for _____. This is making it difficult for me and others to get our office work done. I think it is hurting _____ too."

The following comments from part-time telecommuters substantiate reports that the quality of communication is improved by their working at home part-time:

> "There really is much less trivial communication, but I feel that the resulting conversations are better. More is accomplished in a shorter time."

> "Communication by phone is shorter and more to the point. People don't call to discuss political problems."

"I am not as available to talk with now. When I talk to someone, we immediately cover the necessary points. For meetings and face-to-face conversations, I make notes of what I need to ask and wait until I'm in the office. I think others do the same when they need to see me."

"When I was in the office, someone would drop in and ask a question. Ten minutes later they would be back to ask something they forgot or clear up what I said. Now we get more done with one interruption."

No change in the job tasks or the complexity of the job tasks are reported by the part-time telecommuters. However, part-time telecommuters do report a decrease in task interdependence. This appears to be a result of the division of their job tasks into those that are best suited for the office and those best suited for the home. This separation results in an overall job which is less dependent upon other workers.

Findings of decreased task interdependence do not reveal the entire picture concerning the dependence of the part-time telecommuters upon other workers. Critical incidents indicate that it is necessary to find "someone [in the office] you feel free to call and ask to do something." These contacts range from secretaries to co-workers.

"Take yesterday, _____ called up and needed to see this report we had been working on. They needed it right then. I called [a co-worker] up and asked for help to get the report."

"You've got to have someone. I would be coming into the office all the time if I couldn't rely on someone."

The increased dependence upon an office worker does not involve the performance of the main tasks (as written in job descriptions) of a person's job. This level of interdependence decreased as was mentioned. Instead, the increased interdependence that is reported in the critical incidents relate to the office errands that employees are often called upon to perform. Being at home preempts the telecommuter's ability to perform these errands without the help of an office contact.

Despite the general lack of structural and task effects of telecommuting, some behavioral effects are reported. Part-time telecommuters experience a drop in their identification with the work group. The remoteness of the telecommuting work site strains their intragroup commitment and identification.

"I never see _____ anymore. It's like _____ doesn't belong to the group."

Generally, the lack of intragroup cohesion with telecommuters does not affect group performance.

"_____ isn't here much, but he is extremely competent and always get the work done; so who cares."

Occasionally, the lack of group identification creates problems:

"_____ is in the office on Mondays, and [he/she] always calls our team meeting then. It doesn't matter whether we need to meet or what else is going on; we meet anyway. I think more concern should be paid to the needs of the project team and less to when _____ is not working at home."

Telecommuting does not produce a negative effect upon managerial relations. In fact, better managerial relations and communication are reported by the managers of the part-time telecommuters. They indicate that the level of communication with the telecommuters is probably better than before the telecommuting experiment began.

"In my opinion, I think I know more what _____ is doing now. He is in closer contact than before and wants to make sure I'm aware that he is working and making progress."

The improvement in managerial relations is largely due to two factors. First, the willingness of a manager to allow a worker to telecommute is seen as an expression of trust and confidence. Second, part-time telecommuters make extra efforts to ensure that this trust is not betrayed. Frequent reports and weekly meetings kept them in touch. The part-time telecommuters are aware of the "out of sight — out of mind" phenomena, and they improve vertical relations to offset it..

Regarding job satisfaction, part-time telecommuters report higher satisfaction concerning working alone, but lower satisfaction concerning the ability to direct the actions of others, opportunities for advancement, and office working conditions. Overall, the part-time telecommuters express satisfaction with telecommuting and appreciation for the ability to work from their homes.

"I feel much more satisfied because I am able to complete my paperwork in the quiet of my home, and devote more time to the necessary interactions with other people in the office."

"I am not nearly as upset when people interrupt me when I'm in the office as I was before [working at home]. I have the time now to talk with people and yet I am doing more documentation on the projects."

"There is much less stress in my work now. I really look forward to the days spent in the office because so much work can be done at home without interruptions."

"I really never liked to socialize at the office. I'm a bit of a loner. I feel much more comfortable working at home."

All of the part-time telecommuters indicate that they would like to continue to work at home indefinitely.

"I really can't say that I would ever get tired of this [telecommuting]."

Several telecommuters also indicate that they are less apt to consider other employment because of the telecommuting opportunity.

"It would be difficult to think of taking another job if I couldn't work at home."

Productivity, rated by the participants and their managers, does not decrease for any of the telecommuters during the study. Telecommuting actually appears to strengthen the potential for increased productivity. Some comments concerning productivity are:

"When I am working at home, I can get the same amount of work done in as little as half the time."

"The extra time I found I gained from working at home was very useful. I was able to do several small favors for clients which, had I been working in the office, I could not have done. I think this [doing the favors] has really helped my client relationships."

"Working at home was worth at least two deadlines. Without it [working at home] I feel certain that these deadlines could not have been met."

Technology plays some role in moderating negative behavioral outcomes that are associated with telecommuting. Due to an acquisition problem, some of the part-time telecommuters did not receive a computer terminal until several weeks after beginning the experiment, and this delay produced some interesting observations on the value of computer communication.

"I was feeling a sense of remoteness or not belonging until they installed the terminal. The first day after [getting the terminal], I turned on the system and looked at the users. Simply looking at this list on the screen made me feel a part of the work group. I realized that I was not alone, but in a community of workers."

"I supervise, in a sense, a couple of night programmers. Using the terminal, I can leave them notes and instructions, and they leave me notes. Without it, it's impossible to contact them."

In summary, all of the part-time telecommuters find telecommuting a beneficial work alternative. Part-time telecommuters discover that their homes are quiet, comfortable places to work, and report an increase in the quality of their communications. Part-time telecommuting can increase productivity, especially if it is set as a goal. The only negative outcomes that are reported concerned some loss of identification with their work group, a decline in their opportunities for advancement and their ability to supervise subordinates. Co-workers express some concern over possible favoritism being given to the telecommuters.

Unable Telecommuters

The scenario for the group of telecommuters who are unable to work actively at home is viewed as a subgroup of the part-time telecommuters. All of the unable group are comprised of individuals who would have been classified in the part-time group if they had been able to work actively at home. The unable group is scheduled to work at home an average of two days per week.

A separate scenario of the unable group of telecommuters is developed to point out the problems which prevented this group from actively working at home.

Demographic and Personal Characteristics

The unable group of telecommuters are demographically similar to the part-time telecommuters. They belong to the same organization, Company 2, and their reasons and motivations for wanting to work at home are also similar to the part-time telecommuters. That is, they view the home as a quiet, comfortable work place in which they could be more productive performing mental intensive tasks. None of the unable telecommuters have any children at home. Three of the unable telecommuters are female; one is male.

Overall, it appears that the unable group is somewhat less enthusiastic about working at home, and they do not plan to work at home as many days as the other part-time telecommuters. Two of the unable telecommuters report that they feel obligated to try telecommuting since they were asked by their supervisors.

The unable group of telecommuters are also involved in different types of jobs from those of the part-time telecommuters. These jobs, editor and text developer, do not involve using computer technology, and computer equipment was not installed in the homes of the unable telecommuters. During the experiment, however, word processors were installed in the offices at Company 2, and the unable telecommuters made significant use of these machines in the office.

Telecommuting Experiences

The part-time telecommuters who are unable to telecommute actively report a substantial increase in the need for face-to-face communication during the experimental period. They indicate that this is primarily due to the phases of the projects in which they are working. This increased need for face-to-face communication is given as a major reason for their inability to telecommute actively.

> "This just wasn't a good time. The stages that my projects are in require a lot of meetings and group decisions . . . we're not ready to go into our corners and work yet."

These telecommuters also report an inability to get at references and resources. This problem is also stated as a major reason for their inability to work actively at home. The references and resources needed by text developers and editors are substantial compared to those of the other telecommuting jobs. The materials are not available through a computer network, and this creates problems in carrying them back and forth from home.

> "Parking is so bad I take the bus . . . by the time I gather up the things I need to work at home, I've got both arms full. Then I've got to walk to catch the bus, then walk several blocks from where the bus lets me off."

The use of word processors in the office often forces the telecommuter to come into the office to perform tasks (such as writing) which are well suited for the home. Several participants indicate that having a word processor in their homes which could access documents and references that are stored on the office word processor would help in overcoming the problems concerning access to references and resources.

Except for a general drop in satisfaction with office working conditions, no changes in organizational behavior, job satisfaction, or performance are found among the unable group. Their attitude about working at home declines as it concerns the social isolation which results from working at home. This group experiences several problems associated with feeling remote and being unable to talk with people when they work at home. Overall, it appears that the unable group of telecommuters have higher social needs than the part-time telecommuters.

> "I really do miss the 'pot-lucks' [office parties]. I wish they would only schedule them when I'm here [working in the office]."

Scenario Conclusions

The telecommuting model used in this research indicates that telecommuting is a structural change in an organization that will directly affect the levels of communication and certain other outcomes associated with the increased spatial-physical distance from the organization and its workers. The scenarios presented in this chapter bear out this contention, but more importantly suggest that this effect is largely dependent upon the number of days a telecommuter works at home.

Full-time telecommuters experience a lower level of communication and spend much less time with their work groups. Part-time telecommuters do not experience a decline in communication because their communication needs match the number of days they work at home. Finally, the group of telecommuters who are unable to work actively at home experience an increase in their communication needs which prevents them from working at home according to their plans.

The telecommuting model also suggests that technology will moderate the structural outcome effects of telecommuting. Again, the scenarios support this contention. Technology is able to moderate a loss in some types of communication, and for some jobs it permits remote access to references and resources.

Telecommuters who do not use computer technology in their jobs have more trouble working at home. All of the people who use computers while working at home are able to telecommute as planned. The four telecommuters who are unable to work actively at home do not use a computer system while at home. Use of the computer to provide references and resources, and a lower social need (found among the telecommuters with computer oriented jobs) appear to be the underlying reasons for this association.

The degree to which telecommuting changes the structural outcome variables also affects the degree of change found in a telecommuter's task variables. The jobs of full-time telecommuters contain fewer job tasks and are less enriched. In contrast, the job tasks of the part-time and unable telecommuters do not change. Technology is responsible for moderating the loss of job tasks. It allows a broad range of tasks to be performed at home which otherwise could not have been included in the jobs of the telecommuters.

The behavioral outcomes of the experiment seem to indicate that successful full-time telecommuters are characterized by having a strong need to work at home coupled with only a rational monetary reason to work. Successful part-time telecommuters are characterized by having a quiet, comfortable home in which to work and relatively low social needs. In contrast, the telecommuters who have problems telecommuting appear to be characterized by having relatively high social needs. One of the most discriminating questions, between the part-time and unable telecommuting group, asks if they missed the "pot-lucks" or office parties. Invariably, the part-time telecommuter will laugh and say no, while the unable telecommuter will reply that "yes, that is a real concern."

11

Practical Applications

Several important implications for practice and future telecommuting studies appear in this study. These implications are important not only to researchers interested in telecommuting and the socio-technical effects of technology, but to managers and practitioners interested in designing and implementing telecommuting as a work alternative. This research provides a significant amount of new information concerning the effects of telecommuting and the types of people and jobs that are suitable for telecommuting.

Structure

One of the most important findings of this research is that the structural effects of telecommuting are highly dependent upon the number of days a telecommuter works at home. This in turn affects the types of jobs and people who can successfully work at home, and the extent to which technology can moderate the negative effects of telecommuting.

Telecommuting is not a uniform structural change. It is a varied experience which depends upon the number of days that a telecommuter works at home. Not only must organizations consider whether to allow employees to work at home, but also they must consider the number of days that their employees should work at home.

Full-time telecommuters work under conditions of restricted communication. They do not have the opportunity to "batch" their communication needs until they are in the office, and the telephone is too narrow a communications media to accommodate all of their communication. On the other hand, part-time telecommuters do not experience a significant reduction in communication because they are often able to batch their communication needs until they are in the office.

The management and control of a telecommuter is also determined by the number of days that he works at home. Full-time telecommuters should be managed using more mechanistic methods than their office counterparts. They should be assigned to work on projects with short-term deadlines. While their jobs can remain project-oriented, the scope and length of these projects should be reduced.

The management and control techniques for full-time telecommuters should include frequent phone calls, and a weekly management meeting. Externally driven short-term deadlines and electronic monitoring are useful techniques for managing clerical full-time telecommuters.

Part-time telecommuters can continue to work under the organic management systems found in the office, but should be more closely monitored than their office counterparts. Management of a part-time telecommuter should rely upon defining weekly deliverables and then trusting the telecommuter to do the work. A weekly meeting should be scheduled to review the telecommuter's progress and to set the next week's deliverables.

The organization should provide a key contact person in the office for the part-time telecommuters. This person serves to perform certain office tasks which cannot be done by the telecommuters when they are working at home. Additionally, the organization should develop a scheduling system which accounts for the days that telecommuters are working at home. This system is used to schedule meetings and seminars only on days in which the telecommuter is in the office.

Tasks

The structural changes which occur as a result of telecommuting affect the types of job tasks which are suitable for full-time and part-time telecommuting.

The jobs of full-time telecommuters should be highly dependent upon technology. Without the use of telecommunications and computer technology, the cost of sending work and receiving work cannot be justified. Additionally, the use of technology allows a substantial number of the office job tasks to be transferred to the home. The jobs tasks of full-time telecommuters must also be largely independent of other workers such as secretaries and peers, and their work on team projects should be reduced. Tasks which require complex interpersonal communication such as determining user needs and project planning require many face-to-face meetings and cannot be done by full-time telecommuters. Also, tasks associated with training new workers and building team spirit cannot be expected of full-time telecommuters.

Part-time telecommuters should have jobs where at least half of the tasks require mentally intensive work. The jobs of part-time telecommuters should also be dependent upon computer technology. Because of the cost of placing the required computer equipment in the home and other behavioral requirements, part-time telecommuting is viable only for skilled professional workers.

The number of days that a part-time telecommuter must spend in the office should be determined by the amount of face-to-face interaction required by the telecommuter's job tasks. The level of face-to-face communication is determined by the job tasks and the manner in which the tasks are integrated into the project team effort. Jobs such as editing and writing which appear suitable for telecommuting may not be if they require constant feedback communication from other team members. Additionally, a part-time telecommuter's complex interpersonal communication needs should be capable of being "batched" until the worker is in the office. Work such as "creative deal-making" which often requires immediate complex interpersonal communication is not suitable for part-time telecommuting.

The amount of reference and resource materials which part-time telecommuters must physically transport between the office and home should be minimal. The use of the computer and telecommunications technology to bring most or all references and resources "on-line" is important to successful part-time telecommuting.

People

The structural changes of telecommuting also affect the types of people who are suitable for full-time or part-time telecommuting.

Full-time telecommuting is a successful work alternative when telecommuters have a strong personal need to work at home such as caring for their children. Only an individual who has an important reason for wanting to work at home should be considered as a full-time telecommuter. Additionally, the full-time telecommuter should have only monetary reasons for wanting to work and should not miss the loss of the social interactions associated with the office. As a telecommuter, their job will offer little hope for advancement and will not be as challenging as an office job. However, if their reason for wanting to work at home is sufficient, this will prevail over the negative outcomes of full-time telecommuting and the worker will be satisfied with the telecommuting arrangement.

Part-time telecommuting does not produce as many negative outcomes as full-time telecommuting; therefore, it does not require as strong of a desire to work at home as full-time telecommuting. However, part-time telecommuters will be concerned about their opportunities for advancement and the difficulty of supervising subordinates. They will also experience some alienation and loss of identity concerning their work group. To overcome these negative feelings, part-time telecommuters must feel that their home is a more quiet and comfortable environment for performing mentally intensive writing and planning tasks than the office, and that they are more productive by working at home. The part-time telecommuter's productivity should increase by an amount that is sufficient to overcome the problems of working remotely. They should be achievement oriented, self-disciplined, and self-directed.

Successful part-time telecommuters should also have low social needs. People who do not miss the social interaction of the office are best suited for part-time telecommuting. Individuals who miss the social interactions of the office and are concerned about the isolation of working at home should not be considered for either full-time or part-time telecommuting programs.

Technology

The use of telecommunications and computer technology helps moderate the negative effects of telecommuting but it cannot eliminate them.

Technology can be used to transfer many of the job tasks of telecommuters to the home environment. Additionally, the telephone can accommodate communication needs that are characterized as informational and immediately important to the performance of the job. However, the current state of computer and telecommunications technology cannot accommodate complex interpersonal communication requirements and these must be eliminated from the telecommuter's job or be capable of being batched until the telecommuter is in the office. Telecommuters should be expected to make only limited use of electronic mail and to rely almost exclusively upon communication by telephone.

The technical requirements for a professional who telecommutes include two aspects. First, the home configuration must be adequate to accomplish the job tasks of the telecommuter. Second, the home configuration should be able to perform the functions normally performed by a secretary or office assistant.

These requirements suggest that a personal computer which is capable of performing "executive work station" tasks such as word processing, financial planning, scheduling, and maintaining personal databases is needed. The personal computer will provide the telecommuter with a fast response for most of his work and will produce flexible working hours. The home computer must be able to communicate with the office computers to upload and download documents stored on them as well as run mainframe programs remotely. The home computer should also be capable of being accessed remotely. Therefore, when the telecommuter is not at home he will have the ability to run his personal programs from a remote terminal and to send and receive files. For some telecommuters such as programmers, a character printer in the home will also be needed to obtain printouts.

Because telecommuters rely heavily upon voice communications and there is no secretary to answer the phone while at home, a personal computer which is capable of making extensive use of voice recognition and response technology will further moderate the negative effects of telecommuting. Such a facility should:

- Receive and store telephone calls, and provide appropriate messages based upon the caller.
- Forward the message to the telephone nearest the telecommuter if necessary.
- Receive calls from the telecommuter and execute commands remotely based upon voice recognition.
- Transcribe spoken dictation using voice recognition.
- Automatically schedule appointments and remind the worker of the appointments.

The ability of workers to telecommute part-time will be enhanced as computers are able to assume these tasks normally performed by a secretary or office assistant.

Limitations of the Research

This section considers the limitations of the research which affected the usefulness and generalizations of the findings. The limitations are presented along with the attempts made to control for them.

Sample Size

The small sample size presents problems which affect the statistical analysis and the ability to test the hypotheses. The researcher tried every possible method available to him to increase the sample size, but the current exploratory state of telecommuting and the financial requirements and risks involved limited the success of these efforts. The choice was made to settle for a small sample size using field experiments in organizations rather than a larger sample using a laboratory setting with "make-work" types of tasks.

The small sample size makes classical testing of the hypothesis using statistical procedures suspect. Instead, three approaches to analyzing the data are performed. The statistical analysis is augmented with graphical trends of the measured responses, and interpretation and support for the statistical and graphical findings are provided by subjective observations and critical incidents. The combination of these approaches provides evidence to support or refute a hypothesis and insight into the underlying causes and events which produce the results.

While the small sample size poses many problems concerning the statistics and their validity, it also provides the researcher with an opportunity to work closely with the participants and monitor their experiences. This effort cannot completely overcome the difficulties in testing the hypotheses, but it does provide a foundation upon which future research can be built.

Nonequivalent Groups

The quasi-experimental design that is used in this study does not assign subjects to the treatment and control groups. Instead, telecommuters are selected by mutual agreements between the telecommuters and their organizations. This self-selection bias may affect the research results.

An attempt is made in the selection of control participants to match them with their telecommuting counterparts. This matching process appears to be successful. No differences between the telecommuting and control groups on the demographic variables are found. However, it seems likely that some differences do in fact exist.

Therefore, the experimental design uses pretreatment measures of the response variables to control for differences that are not eliminated by the matching of control participants. Pretreatment responses are used to adjust post-treatment responses using the analysis of covariance statistic.

The combination of matching and pretreatment response adjustment adequately controls for the nonequivalences between the control and treatment groups. However, when the telecommuting group is divided into three subgroups comprised of the full-time, part-time, and unable groups some demographic and personal differences are present. These differences are not controlled, and they limit the conclusions which are drawn about the effects of telecommuting on the subgroups. However, the differences found among the telecommuting groups does provide insight into the demographic and personal characteristics of individuals who have problems adopting telecommuting and those individuals who are likely to self-select themselves into full-time and part-time telecommuting programs.

Alternative Explanations for Differences

The differences that are reported in this research between the telecommuting and control groups, and among the full-time, part-time, and unable telecommuting groups, are viewed as being caused by telecommuting. Aside from sample size problems that may have highlighted differences which in fact do not exist, other alternative explanations for the differences in the measured outcome variables are possible.

One of the alternate explanations for the reported differences can be the discrepancies in demographic variables among the groups. For example, the loss in communication that is reported by the full-time telecommuters, as opposed to the increase in communication that is reported by the part-time telecommuters, can be explained as a result of their differential experiences with telecommuting. This finding may also be a result of the differences between the groups in demographic variables such as sex and children at home. The research attempts to control for these interpretation problems by relying upon observations and critical incidents. For example, observation and critical incidents indicate that the communication loss is indeed a result of telecommuting full-time. However, subjective evidence cannot completely rule out the alternate explanation of demographic differences.

A second explanation of the differences among the groups concerns certain organizational or situational events that occurred during the course of the experiments. For example, the telecommuters in the part-time and unable groups all worked in Company 2, while the full-time telecommuters worked in the other organizations. During the last month of the experiment, the area in which the telecommuters in Company 2 worked was reorganized. This event affected the telecommuters in Company 2 for several weeks. Since the full-time groups did not experience this reorganization, the differences that were found between these groups can be attributed to the reorganization and not to telecommuting. Again, the use of subjective observations and critical incidents is relied upon to control for this type of alternative explanation.

While alternative explanations for the observed results cannot be ruled out, the use of observations and critical incidents helps to control for them. Also, in several instances the demographic and situational variables do interact with the telecommuting results. These interactions are presented in the scenarios, and they provide important information concerning the conditional effects of telecommuting.

Measurement Instruments

Studies that involve organizational and behavioral constructs rely upon the quality of the instruments that are used to operationalize those constructs. This problem is considered by the researcher to be the most serious limitation of this study.

The lack of prior research concerning telecommuting results in a large number of outcome variables which are hypothesized to be affected by telecommuting. Instruments to measure these outcome variables are either nonexistent or unknown to the researcher. Only one instrument, the Minnesota Satisfaction Questionnaire, has a history of use and has been pretested for reliability and validity. The other instruments are modified portions of questionnaires proposed by other researchers or questions developed by the researcher.

Unfortunately, several of the participating organizations were unwilling to postpone the start of their telecommuting experiment while the researcher pretested the instruments. Therefore, untested instruments were used during the pretreatment time period. The instruments were then modified from feedback gained during the pretreatment period. While many of the questions in the revised instrument appear reliable, several are not and have to be discarded. In other cases, the construct validity of a question is suspect.

The use of observations and critical incidents helps to control for some of the instrumentation problems. The subjective evidence is useful and produces meaningful results in many cases which otherwise would not have been interpretable. However, the problem remains a major limitation to the usefulness and interpretability of the results.

Randomness of the Sample

Generalizations drawn from the research results in this study depend on the sample being representative of the population. The nature of the field experiment and the infant state of telecommuting makes random sampling from the population of organizations, jobs, and workers impossible. Therefore, generalizing beyond this experiment is limited.

The telecommuting results found in this experiment can only be interpreted within the limited situations and organizations in which they are observed. However, observations and critical incidents illustrate how many of the organizational, job, and worker contingencies affect the results. This additional information provides insight into the mechanisms whereby telecommuting affects organizational and behavioral outcomes, and whether the results observed in this experiment will likely occur in different jobs and organizations.

Overcoming the inability of this research to generalize the results outside of the situations in this experiment is left to future research. However, the information obtained in this experiment provides a framework and some necessary preliminary information for pursuing that future research.

Closing Remarks

This study is an exploratory investigation into the organizational and behavioral effects of telecommuting. Telecommuting is shown to have a varied effect upon organizational and behavioral variables depending upon the number of days a telecommuter works at home. The data also suggests that certain job task characteristics and personal characteristics will interact with telecommuting to determine the organizational and behavioral effects.

An examination of the hypotheses and scenarios suggests that full-time telecommuting produces many negative organizational and behavioral effects. These effects can be surmounted if the telecommuter has a strong desire to work at home, and the organization is willing to restrict the job tasks of the telecommuter. On the other hand, part-time telecommuting does not involve the negative organization and behavioral effects of full-time telecommuting. However, part-time telecommuting appears suitable only for skilled professional workers who do not miss the social interactions found in the office environment and who have quiet and comfortable homes which are well suited to the performance of mentally intensive tasks.

Generally, these results do not support the contention that full-time telecommuting is likely to become a widespread work alternative. The population of potential full-time telecommuters will be limited to home-bound individuals who have a strong need to work at home. Also, the inability of technology to fully moderate the negative outcomes of full-time telecommuting will limit the types of jobs that can be considered. Finally, there is little evidence in this study to suggest that full-time telecommuting can increase productivity by increasing performance. Productivity can only be increased for full-time telecommuters by decreasing their labor costs such as eliminating benefits or paying telecommuters contract wages.

Part-time telecommuting holds more promise than full-time telecommuting and widespread acceptance of this form of telecommuting may indeed occur as the technology of the "executive work station" evolves. As this technology is made available, workers will become less dependent upon other workers such as secretaries and office assistants in accomplishing their jobs and their ability to work at home several days a week without negative consequences is increasingly possible.

Appendix A

Data Gathering Instruments

Exhibit 1

Pretelecommuting Interview

PRIMARY SUBJECTS INTERVIEW QUESTIONNAIRE

Instructions

Below are question on organizational and behavioral factors which may be affected by telecommuting. During the interview, the space on the answer sheet which describes your response will be entered by the interviewer. For example, on the first question the number to be filled in on the answer sheet that best describes the amount of time you spend communicating face-to-face with someone during work will be recorded as follows:

1.11   What percent of the time do you spend communicating face-to-face with someone during work?

1	2	3	4	5	6	7	8	9
0-11%	22%	33%	44%	55%	66%	77%	88%	99%
of your time is spent communicating face-to-face with someone during work.				of your time is spent communicating face-to-face with someone during work			of your time is spent communicating face-to-face with someone during work.	

1.00 Communication
1.10 General

1.11   What percent of the time do you spend communicating face-to-face with someone during work?

1.12   What percent of the time do you spend communicating with people outside your work group?

1.13   What percent of the time do you receive conflicting information about your job or the organization?

1.20 Specific-horizontal

1.21   To what extent do you have useful discussions with other group members on job related subjects (such as on work problems, how to resolve personal conflicts, and so forth)?

1.22   To what extent do you have discussions with other group members on non-job related subjects (such as politics, sports, etc)?

1.30 Specific-Upward

1.31 What percent of your time do you spend talking to your supervisor about your performance?

1.32 What percent of your time do you spend talking to your supervisor about yourself and your problems?

1.33 What percent of your time do you spend talking to your supervisor about others and their problems?

1.34 What percent of your time do you spend talking to your supervisor about organizational practices and policies?

1.35 What percent of your time do you spend talking to your supervisor about what needs to be done and how it can be done?

1.40 Specific-Downward

1.41 What percent of your time do you spend giving specific task or job instructions to people who work for you?

1.42 What percent of your time do you spend giving information to produce an understanding of the job and its relation to other organizational tasks (i.e., job rationale)?

1.43 What percent of your time do you spend providing information about organizational procedures and practices to people who work for your?

1.44 What percent of your time do you spend giving subordinates feedback on their performance?

1.45 What percent of your time do you spend providing information about the goals and mission of the group and/or organization?

2.00 Spatial-Physical Barriers

2.11 What percentage of members of your work group are located so far away that you cannot carry on a normal conversation without shouting or going out of your way?

2.12 What percentage of members are located so you don't have direct eye contact with them unless you turn around or move from your regular position or office?

2.13 What percentage of time do you have a question but because you are located away from the person who could answer that question, you do not ask?

2.14 What percentage of time are you unable to talk with someone because nobody is around to talk to?

2.15 What percentage of the time are you unable to get at reference or resource materials when you need them to do your job?

3.00 Work Flows

3.11 What percentage of your work are you dependent upon other members of your work group (that is, it is necessary to coordinate your job with what they are doing)?

3.12 Inventories or other buffers between positions may permit one to continue to work when breakdowns occur or others are absent. Under normal conditions, what percent of your work is so interrelated that you cannot continue to work from one day or longer when individuals are absent from the group or breakdowns and other stoppages occur?

4.00 Task Complexity

4.11 In some jobs, things are unpredictable--if you do something to solve a problem, you don't know what will happen. What percent of the time are you unsure on how things will work as expected?

4.12 What percent of the time are you at a loss about whom to go to for reliable help when you cannot solve a problem?

5.00 Organizational Behavior
5.10 Individual Behavior

5.11 To what extent are you committed to your work (like trying to do the job well and taking pride in your work)?

5.12 What percentage of the time do you try to meet work standards, or other measures of a full day's work?

5.13 To what extent do you automatically increase your work pace and shorten work breaks as work pressure increases?

5.14 To what degree do you assume job responsibility (such as trying to improve methods and solve work problems?

5.15 What percentage of your time do you try and develop your skills and abilities to do a better job?

5.16 What percentage of the time do you feel contented, (rather than frustrated) in trying to do your job?

5.17 To what degree do you have a sense of achievement in performing your job (such as getting a kick out of doing good work)?

5.18 What percentage of the time are you on the job?

5.19 To what extent do you think of staying on your job (that is, your aren't thinking of quitting, or asking for a transfer)?

5.20 Intragroup

5.21 What percentage of the members in your work group do you have confidence in and trust?

5.22 What percentage of the time do members of your group help you when assistance is needed without being asked?

5.23 To what degree do you identify with your work group (such as feeling part of the group, and wishing to remain in the group)?

5.30 Vertical

5.31 To what extent does your supervisor show he/she has trust and confidence in you?

5.32 To what degree do you have trust and confidence in him/her?

5.33 When information is requested by your supervisor, to what extent do your provide accurate and complete data?

5.34 What percentage of the time is it unnecessary for you to withhold and distort information from you supervisor for your own self protection?

5.35 To what extent do you bring job problems to his/her attention?

5.36 To what degree do you volunteer useful information to him/her on personnel problems, group conflict, and other types of human relations problems?

5.37 To what extent do you have a sense of being a part of your supervisor's team?

5.38 What percentage of the time do your accept decisions of your supervisor? (For example, do you implement his/her orders and requests by interpreting both what his intention is as well as what he/she actually says)?

6.00 Technology Usage
6.10 Phone Usage
6.11 What percentage of your communications with other group members or co-workers is by the phone?
6.12 What percentage of your communications with your supervisor is by phone?
6.13 What percentage of your communications with people who work for you is by phone?
6.14 What percentage of your communications with people who use your work is by phone?
6.15 What percentage of your work is dependent upon using the phone?

6.20 Mainframe Computer Usage
6.21 What percentage of your communications with other group members or co-workers is facilitated by the organization's computer?
6.22 What percentage of your communications with your supervisor is facilitated by the organization's computer?
6.23 What percentage of your communications with people who work for you is facilitated by the organization's computer?
6.24 What percentage of your communications with people who use your work is facilitated by the organization's computer?
6.25 What percentage of your work is dependent upon using the organization's computer?

6.30 Terminal or Micro-computer
6.31 What percentage of your communications with other group members or co-workers is facilitated by the terminal (or micro-computer)?
6.32 What percentage of your communications with your supervisor is facilitated by the terminal (or micro-computer)?
6.33 What percentage of your communications with people who work for you is facilitated by the terminal (or micro-computer)?
6.34 What percentage of your communications with people who use your work is facilitated by the terminal (or micro-computer)?
6.35 What percentage of your work is dependent upon using the terminal (or micro-computer)?

6.40 Applications such as Electronic Mail, TSO, etc.
6.41 What percentage of your communications with other group members or co-workers is facilitated by applications such as electronic mail, TSO, etc.?
6.42 What percentage of your communications with your supervisor is facilitated by applications such as electronic mail, TSO, etc.?
6.43 What percentage of your communications with people who work for you is facilitated by applications such as electronic mail, TSO, etc.?
6.44 What percentage of your communications with people who use your your is is facilitated by applications such as electronic mail, TSO, etc.?
6.45 What percentage of your work is dependent upon using applications such as electronic mail, TSO, etc.?

Exhibit 2

Attitude towards Working at Home Questionnaire

ATTITUDE QUESTIONNAIRE ON WORKING AT HOME

The purpose of this questionnaire is to gather the opinions and attitudes of workers concerning working at home. Based on pre-test experience, approximately ten minutes are necessary to complete the questionnaire. Participation is voluntary and all replies will remain confidential. If you have any questions contact:

Reagan Ramsower, Research Associate MIS Research Center
office: (612) 373-7993   home: (612) 588-0074

I.   WORK INFORMATION

1. How many hours per week, on the average, do you spend working on:

				HOURS PER WEEK			
a. Systems analysts activities?	0	1-5	6-10	11-15	16-20	21-25	25+
b. Detailed system design activities?	0	1-5	6-10	11-15	16-20	21-25	25+
c. Programming and Procedure writing activities?	0	1-5	6-10	11-15	16-20	21-25	25+
d. System Final test and conversion activites?	0	1-5	6-10	11-15	16-20	21-25	25+
e. System Maintenance activities?	0	1-5	6-10	11-15	16-20	21-25	25+
f. Other activities? Please describe.	0	1-5	6-10	11-15	16-20	21-25	25+

_____

2. At present, what percent of time do you spend working alone on activities? _____ %

3. At present, how many hours per week do you spend working at home:

				HOURS PER WEEK			
a. During regular work hours?	0	1-5	6-10	11-15	16-20	21-25	25+
b. Not during regular work hours?	0	1-5	6-10	11-15	16-20	21-25	25+

II.   PERCEPTIONS OF WORKING AT HOME

Instructions: Please respond to the following questions with respect to your current work situation. Circle your response and use the following scale positions. If your are uncertain or think that it is neither, or the question does not apply, circle scale position 4 .

TERM X	1	2	3	4	5	6	7	TERM Y
	Extremely X	Quite X	Slightly X	Uncertain Neither	Slightly Y	Quite Y	Extremely Y	

4. Given your current work situation:

		How good or bad would you rate the following outcomes?	What is the likelyhood that your working at home during the next 6 months would lead to the following outcomes?
a.	Reduce the frequency of interrruptions in your work.	1 2 3 4 5 6 7 good bad	1 2 3 4 5 6 7 likely unlikely
b.	Increase your control over starting and ending a unit of work.	1 2 3 4 5 6 7 good bad	1 2 3 4 5 6 7 likely unlikely
c.	Decrease your contact with your supervisor and co-workers.	1 2 3 4 5 6 7 good bad	1 2 3 4 5 6 7 likely unlikely
d.	Decrease your contact with the people who will use the results of your work.	1 2 3 4 5 6 7 good bad	1 2 3 4 5 6 7 likely unlikely
e.	Decrease your access to reference materials or documentation.	1 2 3 4 5 6 7 good bad	1 2 3 4 5 6 7 likely unlikely
f.	Decrease the time and strain which results from commuting to work.	1 2 3 4 5 6 7 good bad	1 2 3 4 5 6 7 likely unlikely
g.	Provide a quiet atmosphere to work in?	1 2 3 4 5 6 7 good bad	1 2 3 4 5 6 7 likely unlikely
h.	Provide a casual atmosphere to work in?	1 2 3 4 5 6 7 good bad	1 2 3 4 5 6 7 likely unlikely
i.	Increase the amount of time spent with your family.	1 2 3 4 5 6 7 good bad	1 2 3 4 5 6 7 likely unlikely
j.	Improve your work productivity.	1 2 3 4 5 6 7 good bad	1 2 3 4 5 6 7 likely unlikely

5. In terms of your current work situation, what are the advantages and disadvantages of your work at home during the next six months?
ADVANTAGES: _____

DISADVANTAGES: _____

6. Given your preference, how many days per week would you stay at home to work during the next six months?

___ # days

7. Overall, how good would working at home during the next six months be for you?

1 2 3 4 5 6 7
good   bad

8. Given your current work situation:

To what degree are the following for or against you working at home during the next six months?

How important is it to do what the following think you should do?

a. Your supervisor

1 2 3 4 5 6 7
for   against

1 2 3 4 5 6 7
important unimportant

b. Your co-workers

1 2 3 4 5 6 7
for   against

1 2 3 4 5 6 7
important unimportant

c. Your company

1 2 3 4 5 6 7
for   against

1 2 3 4 5 6 7
important unimportant

d. Your spouse

1 2 3 4 5 6 7
for   against

1 2 3 4 5 6 7
important unimportant

9. Why are these group for or against you working at home during the next six months? Are there other groups or people that your influence your decision to work at home?

10. Overall, to what degree are the people most important to you and your job, for or against you working at home during the next six months?

1 2 3 4 5 6 7
for   against

11. Given your current work situation, what is the likelihood that you will be working at home during the next six months?

1 2 3 4 5 6 7
likely   unlikely

12. What conditions make it difficult (or easy) for you to stay home and work?

_____

_____

III. PERSONAL INFORMATION

13. How long have you worked:
    a. In your current position? _____ # years
    b. In your company? _____ # years

14. How old are you? _____ #years.

15. What sex are you? ___ Male   ___ Female

16. What level of education have you completed (check those that apply)?

    ___ High School Diploma   ___ Undergraduate college coursework   ___ Graduate college degree

    ___ Vocational institute   ___ Undergraduate college degree   ___ Other, please specify: _____

17. How many people are you currently living with at home (not including yourself)? _____ # people

18. If you have children living at home with you, what are their ages? ____, ____, ____, ____, ____, # years

19. What is your current one way commuting distance from home to work? _____ # miles.

Exhibit 3

Working at Home Interview

INTERVIEW FOR PARTICIPANTS WHO ARE WORKING AT HOME

1. Why did you want to work at home?

2. How many days have you been working at home?

3. How has it worked?

4. What has been the most significant advantages?
   Would you give some specific incidents?

5. What has been the most significant disadvantages?
   Would you give some specific incidents?

6. How have you divided your work?
   Would you give some specific incidents?

7. What about stress? Has there been more or less?

8. What about social interaction? professional interaction?

9. How did your communication with co-workers change?
   Would you give some specific incidents?

10. How did your communication with you supervisor change?
    Would you give some specific incidents?

11. How did your communication with subordinates change?
    Would you give some specific incidents?

12. Did you find you physical seperation a problem for
    meetings? Resources?
    Would you give some specific incidents?

13. Is your job less dependent upon others?
    Would you give some specific incidents?

14. Is your job less or more complex or difficult at home?
    Would you give some specific incidents?

15. Did you feel isolated from the organization at home?
    Co-workers? Job?
    Would you give some specific incidents?

16. How did the relationship with your co-workers change?
    Supervisor? Subordinates?
    Would you give some specific incidents?

17. How did you develop self-discipline? against family, weather, other distractions?
    Would you give some specific incidents?

18. Did you use the phone more? Terminal?
    Was this important for you to be able to work at home?
    Would you give some specific incidents?

19. What types of communication did you use the phone for? Terminal for?
    Would you give some specific incidents?

20. How did you job change when you worked at home? The mix of tasks?
    Would you give some specific incidents?

21. What effect did this have on your performance? more or less projects etc.
    Would you give some specific incidents?

22. What effect did this have on your visibility? Promotability?
    Would you give some specific incidents?

23. What effect did this have on your job satisfaction?
    Would you give some specific incidents?

24. Effect on family? Space in you home?

25. How much was it worth for you to be able to work at home?

26. What sort of training would be good for people who want to work at home?
    Would you give some specific incidents?

27. What is the difference between working after hours at home and this concept of working at home?
    Would you give some specific incidents?

Exhibit 4

Working at Home Questionnaire

WORKING AT HOME QUESTIONNAIRE - SECTION I

Instructions

Below are question on your perceptions and feelings about your organization and the time you spend communicating with people. Please circle the number on the answer sheet which best describes your perception or feeling. For example, on the first question circle the number which best describes the amount of time you spent communicating face-to-face with someone during work in the last 3 months. Use the words under the numbers to help anchor your response with your perception or feeling. If you do not wish to reply to a particular question or you feel that question does not apply to you, please leave that question blank. Feel free to make comments beside the questions.

1.11   During the last 3 months how much of your time did you spend communicating face-to-face with someone during work?

0	1	2	3	4	5	6	7	8	9
NONE	Very LITTLE of your time was spent communicating face-to-face with someone during work.		SOME		A MODERATE amount of your time was spent communicating face-to-face with someone during work		CONSIDERABLE		An EXTENSIVE amount of your time was spent communicating face-to-face with someone during work.

1.00 COMMUNICATION
In General

1.11   During the last 3 months how much of your work time did you spend communicating face-to-face with someone during work?

0	1	2	3	4	5	6	7	8	9
NONE	LITTLE		SOME		MODERATE		CONSIDERABLE		EXTENSIVE

1.12   During the last 3 months how much of your work time did you spend communicating with people outside your work group? (your work group consists of peers and co-workers)

0	1	2	3	4	5	6	7	8	9
NONE	LITTLE		SOME		MODERATE		CONSIDERABLE		EXTENSIVE

1.13   During the last 3 months how much of your communication contained conflicting information about your job or the organization?

       0   1   2   3   4   5   6   7   8   9
       NONE   LITTLE   SOME   MODERATE   CONSIDERABLE   EXTENSIVE

Communications with peers and co-workers (i.e. group members)

1.21   During the last 3 months, how much of your work time was involved in discussions with other group members on job related subjects (such as on work problems, how to resolve personal conflicts, and so forth)?

       0   1   2   3   4   5   6   7   8   9
       NONE   LITTLE   SOME   MODERATE   CONSIDERABLE   EXTENSIVE

1.22   During the last 3 months, how much of your work time was involved in discussions with other group members on non-job related subjects (such as politics, sports, etc)?

       0   1   2   3   4   5   6   7   8   9
       NONE   LITTLE   SOME   MODERATE   CONSIDERABLE   EXTENSIVE

Communications with your supervisor

1.31   During the last 3 months, how much time did you spend talking to your supervisor about your performance (both formally and informally)?

       0   1   2   3   4   5   6   7   8   9
       NONE   LITTLE   SOME   MODERATE   CONSIDERABLE   EXTENSIVE

1.32   During the last 3 months, how much time did you spend talking to your supervisor about yourself and your problems (both work related and non-work related)?

       0   1   2   3   4   5   6   7   8   9
       NONE   LITTLE   SOME   MODERATE   CONSIDERABLE   EXTENSIVE

1.33 During the last 3 months, how much time did you spend talking to your supervisor about others and their problems (both work related and non-work related)?

0	1	2	3	4	5	6	7	8	9
NONE	LITTLE		SOME		MODERATE		CONSIDERABLE		EXTENSIVE

1.34 During the last 3 months, how much time did you spend talking to your supervisor about organizational practices and policies?

0	1	2	3	4	5	6	7	8	9
NONE	LITTLE		SOME		MODERATE		CONSIDERABLE		EXTENSIVE

1.35 During the last 3 months, how much time did you spend talking to your supervisor about what needs to be done and how it can be done?

0	1	2	3	4	5	6	7	8	9
NONE	LITTLE		SOME		MODERATE		CONSIDERABLE		EXTENSIVE

Communications with people who perform work for you (OMIT questions 1.41 - 1.45 if no one performs work for you)

1.41 During the last 3 months, how much time did you spend giving task or job instructions to people who perform work for you?

0	1	2	3	4	5	6	7	8	9
NONE	LITTLE		SOME		MODERATE		CONSIDERABLE		EXTENSIVE

1.42 During the last 3 months, how much time did you spend giving information to produce an understanding of the job and its relation to other organizational tasks (i.e., job rationale) to people who perform work for you?

0	1	2	3	4	5	6	7	8	9
NONE	LITTLE		SOME		MODERATE		CONSIDERABLE		EXTENSIVE

1.43 During the last 3 months, how much time did you spend providing information about organizational procedures and practices to people who perform work for you?

0	1	2	3	4	5	6	7	8	9
NONE	LITTLE		SOME		MODERATE		CONSIDERABLE		EXTENSIVE

1.44 During the last 3 months, how much time did you spend giving the people who perform work for you feedback on their performance?

0	1	2	3	4	5	6	7	8	9
NONE	LITTLE		SOME		MODERATE		CONSIDERABLE		EXTENSIVE

1.45 During the last 3 months, how much time did you spend providing information about the goals and mission of the group and/or organization to people who peform work for you?

0	1	2	3	4	5	6	7	8	9
NONE	LITTLE		SOME		MODERATE		CONSIDERABLE		EXTENSIVE

SPATIAL AND PHYSICAL BARRIERS

2.11 During the last 3 months, how often were you located so far away from members of your work group that you could not carry on a conversation without using the telephone (or terminal) or traveling to another location?

0	1	2	3	4	5	6	7	8	9
NONE	LITTLE		SOME		MODERATE		CONSIDERABLE		EXTENSIVE

2.12 During the last 3 months, how often were you unable to have a face-to-face conversation, when such a conversation was needed, because you were physically located away from the person(s) to talk with?

0	1	2	3	4	5	6	7	8	9
NONE	LITTLE		SOME		MODERATE		CONSIDERABLE		EXTENSIVE

2.13 During the last 3 months, how often did you have a question but because you were located away from the person who could answer that question, you did not ask?

0	1	2	3	4	5	6	7	8	9
NONE	LITTLE		SOME		MODERATE		CONSIDERABLE		EXTENSIVE

2.14 During the last 3 months, how often were you unable to talk with someone (both work related and non-work related) because no one was around to talk to?

0	1	2	3	4	5	6	7	8	9
NONE	LITTLE		SOME		MODERATE		CONSIDERABLE		EXTENSIVE

2.15 During the last 3 months, how often were you unable to get at reference or resource materials when you needed them to do your job because they were in a different physical location from you?

0	1	2	3	4	5	6	7	8	9
NONE	LITTLE		SOME		MODERATE		CONSIDERABLE		EXTENSIVE

WORK FLOWS AMONG PEERS AND CO-WORKERS (I.E. WORK GROUP)

3.11 During the last 3 months, how much of your work was dependent upon other members of your work group (that is, it was necessary to coordinate your job with what they were doing)?

0	1	2	3	4	5	6	7	8	9
NONE	LITTLE		SOME		MODERATE		CONSIDERABLE		EXTENSIVE

3.12 During the last 3 months, how much of your work was so interrelated that you could not continue to work on a particular project or report when an individual was absent or could not be reached, or an equipment breakdown occured? (Note: you may have continued to work, but on a different project or report)

0	1	2	3	4	5	6	7	8	9
NONE	LITTLE		SOME		MODERATE		CONSIDERABLE		EXTENSIVE

TASK COMPLEXITY OF YOUR JOB

4.11 In some jobs, things are unpredictable--if you do something to solve a problem, you don't know what will happen. During the last 3 months, how often were you unsure on whether things would work as expected?

0	1	2	3	4	5	6	7	8	9
NONE	LITTLE		SOME		MODERATE		CONSIDERABLE		EXTENSIVE

4.12 During the last 3 months, how often were you at a loss about whom to go to for reliable help when you could not solve a problem?

0	1	2	3	4	5	6	7	8	9
NONE	LITTLE		SOME		MODERATE		CONSIDERABLE		EXTENSIVE

ORGANIZATION FEELINGS AND PERCEPTIONS
Feelings about your job

5.11 During the last 3 months, to what extent were you committed to your work (i.e. trying to do the job well and taking pride in your work)?

0	1	2	3	4	5	6	7	8	9
NEVER	SELDOM		SOMETIMES		OFTEN		USUALLY		ALWAYS

5.12 During the last 3 months, to what extent did you work by some type of work standard (i.e. some measure of a full day's work)? (NOTE: This standard may have been set for you, or you may have set it yourself)

0	1	2	3	4	5	6	7	8	9
NEVER	SELDOM		SOMETIMES		OFTEN		USUALLY		ALWAYS

5.13 During the last 3 months, to what extent did you automatically increase your work pace and shorten your work breaks when work pressures increased?

0	1	2	3	4	5	6	7	8	9
NEVER	SELDOM		SOMETIMES		OFTEN		USUALLY		ALWAYS

5.14 During the last 3 months, to what extent did you try to improve work methods to solve work problems?

0	1	2	3	4	5	6	7	8	9
NEVER	SELDOM		SOMETIMES		OFTEN		USUALLY		ALWAYS

5.15 During the last 3 months, how much time did you spend trying to develop your skills and abilities to do a better job?

0	1	2	3	4	5	6	7	8	9
NEVER	SELDOM		SOMETIMES		OFTEN		USUALLY		ALWAYS

5.16 During the last 3 months, to what extent did you feel contented, (rather than frustrated) in trying to do your job?

0	1	2	3	4	5	6	7	8	9
NEVER	SELDOM		SOMETIMES		OFTEN		USUALLY		ALWAYS

5.17 During the last 3 months, to what extent did you have a sense of achievement in performing your job (such as getting a kick out of doing good work)?

0	1	2	3	4	5	6	7	8	9
NEVER	SELDOM		SOMETIMES		OFTEN		USUALLY		ALWAYS

5.18 During the last 3 months, to what extent were you acutally working while on the job (i.e. exclude extra breaks for coffee, social discussion etc)?

0	1	2	3	4	5	6	7	8	9
NEVER	SELDOM		SOMETIMES		OFTEN		USUALLY		ALWAYS

5.19 During the last 3 months, to what extent did you think of quitting or asking for a transfer?

0	1	2	3	4	5	6	7	8	9
NEVER	SELDOM		SOMETIMES		OFTEN		USUALLY		ALWAYS

Feelings about your peers and co-workers (i.e. work group)

5.21 During the last 3 months, how many of the members in your work group did you have confidence in and trust?

0	1	2	3	4	5	6	7	8	9
NONE	FEW		SOME		HALF		MOST		ALL

5.22 During the last 3 months, to what extent were you close enough to the members of your work group so that they knew when you needed assistance and offered their help?

0	1	2	3	4	5	6	7	8	9
NEVER	SELDOM		SOMETIMES		OFTEN		USUALLY		ALWAYS

5.23 During the last 3 months, to what extent did you identify with your work group (such as feeling part of the group, and wishing to remain in the group)?

0	1	2	3	4	5	6	7	8	9
NEVER	SELDOM		SOMETIMES		OFTEN		USUALLY		ALWAYS

Feelings about your supervisor

5.31 During the last 3 months, to what extent did your supervisor show he/she had trust and confidence in you?

0	1	2	3	4	5	6	7	8	9
NEVER	SELDOM		SOMETIMES		OFTEN		USUALLY		ALWAYS

5.32 During the last 3 months, to what extent did you have trust and confidence in your supervisor?

0	1	2	3	4	5	6	7	8	9
NEVER	SELDOM		SOMETIMES		OFTEN		USUALLY		ALWAYS

5.33 During the last 3 months, when information was requested by your supervisor, to what extent did your provide accurate and complete data?

0	1	2	3	4	5	6	7	8	9
NEVER	SELDOM		SOMETIMES		OFTEN		USUALLY		ALWAYS

5.34 During the last 3 months, to what extent was it necessary for you to withhold and/or distort information from you supervisor for your own self protection?

0	1	2	3	4	5	6	7	8	9
NEVER	SELDOM		SOMETIMES		OFTEN		USUALLY		ALWAYS

5.35 During the last 3 months, to what extent did you bring job problems to the attention of your supervisor?

0	1	2	3	4	5	6	7	8	9
NEVER	SELDOM		SOMETIMES		OFTEN		USUALLY		ALWAYS

5.36 During the last 3 months, to what extent did you volunteer information to your supervisor on personnel problems, group conflict, or other types of <u>human relations</u> problems?

0	1	2	3	4	5	6	7	8	9
NEVER	SELDOM		SOMETIMES		OFTEN		USUALLY		ALWAYS

5.37 During the last 3 months, to what extent did you have a sense of being a part of your supervisor's team?

0	1	2	3	4	5	6	7	8	9
NEVER	SELDOM		SOMETIMES		OFTEN		USUALLY		ALWAYS

5.38 During the last 3 months, to what extent did you totally accept the decisions of your supervisor implementing both the order or request as well as the intention?

0	1	2	3	4	5	6	7	8	9
NEVER	SELDOM		SOMETIMES		OFTEN		USUALLY		ALWAYS

USING TECHNOLOGY TO COMMUNICATE
Using the Telephone

6.11 During the last 3 months, how much of your communications with other group members was by the phone?

0	1	2	3	4	5	6	7	8	9
NONE	LITTLE		SOME		MODERATE		CONSIDERABLE		EXTENSIVE

6.12 During the last 3 months, how much of your communications with your supervisor was by phone?

0	1	2	3	4	5	6	7	8	9
NONE	LITTLE		SOME		MODERATE		CONSIDERABLE		EXTENSIVE

6.13 During the last 3 months, how much of your communications with people who perform work for you was by phone? (Omit if no one performs work for you)

0	1	2	3	4	5	6	7	8	9
NONE	LITTLE		SOME		MODERATE		CONSIDERABLE		EXTENSIVE

6.14 During the last 3 months, how much of your communications with people who use your work (i.e. clients, co-workers, peers etc.) was by phone?

0	1	2	3	4	5	6	7	8	9
NONE	LITTLE		SOME		MODERATE		CONSIDERABLE		EXTENSIVE

6.15 During the last 3 months, how much of your work was dependent upon using the phone?

0	1	2	3	4	5	6	7	8	9
NONE	LITTLE		SOME		MODERATE		CONSIDERABLE		EXTENSIVE

Using the Terminal or Computer

6.21 During the last 3 months, how much of your communications with other group members or co-workers was by a computer terminal?

0	1	2	3	4	5	6	7	8	9
NONE	LITTLE		SOME		MODERATE		CONSIDERABLE		EXTENSIVE

6.22 During the last 3 months, how much of your communications with your supervisor was by a computer terminal?

0	1	2	3	4	5	6	7	8	9
NONE	LITTLE		SOME		MODERATE		CONSIDERABLE		EXTENSIVE

6.23 During the last 3 months, how much of your communications with people who perform work for you was by a computer terminal? (Omit if no one performs work for you)

0	1	2	3	4	5	6	7	8	9
NONE	LITTLE		SOME		MODERATE		CONSIDERABLE		EXTENSIVE

6.24 During the last 3 months, how much of your communications with people who use your work (i.e. clients, co-workers, peers, etc.) was by a computer terminal?

0	1	2	3	4	5	6	7	8	9
NONE	LITTLE		SOME		MODERATE		CONSIDERABLE		EXTENSIVE

6.25 During the last 3 months, how much of your work was dependent upon using a computer terminal?

0	1	2	3	4	5	6	7	8	9
NONE	LITTLE		SOME		MODERATE		CONSIDERABLE		EXTENSIVE

WORKING AT HOME QUESTIONNAIRE - SECTION II

Instructions: The purpose of this section is to gather you opinions and attitudes concerning working at home. Please respond to the following questions with respect to your current work situation. Circle your response and use the following scale positions. If you are uncertain or think that it is neither, or the question does not apply, circle scale position 4 .

TERM X						
1	2	3	4	5	6	7
Extremely X	Quite X	Slightly X	Uncertain Neither	Slightly Y	Quite Y	Extremely Y

TERM Y

1. Given your current work situation:

How good or bad would you rate the following outcomes?

What is the likelihood that your working at home during the next 3 months would lead to the following outcomes?

	GOOD					BAD		LIKELY					UNLIKELY	
a. Reduce the frequency of interruptions in your work.	1	2	3	4	5	6	7	1	2	3	4	5	6	7
b. Increase your control over starting and ending a unit of work.	1	2	3	4	5	6	7	1	2	3	4	5	6	7
c. Decrease your contact with your supervisor and co-workers.	1	2	3	4	5	6	7	1	2	3	4	5	6	7
d. Decrease your contact with the people who will use the results of your work.	1	2	3	4	5	6	7	1	2	3	4	5	6	7
e. Decrease your access to reference materials or documentation.	1	2	3	4	5	6	7	1	2	3	4	5	6	7
f. Decrease the time and/or strain which results from commuting to work.	1	2	3	4	5	6	7	1	2	3	4	5	6	7
g. Provide a quiet atmosphere to work in?	1	2	3	4	5	6	7	1	2	3	4	5	6	7
h. Provide a casual atmosphere to work in?	1	2	3	4	5	6	7	1	2	3	4	5	6	7
i. Increase the amount of time spent with	1	2	3	4	5	6	7	1	2	3	4	5	6	7
j. Improve your work productivity.	1	2	3	4	5	6	7	1	2	3	4	5	6	7

2. In terms of your current work situation, what are the advantages and disadvantages for you to be working at home during the next three months?

   ADVANTAGES:

   DISADVANTAGES:

3. Given your preference, how many days per week would you stay at home to work during the next three months?

   _____ # days

4. Overall, how good would working at home during the next three months be for you?

   1   2   3   4   5   6   7
   GOOD   BAD

5. Given your current work situation:

   To what degree are the following for or against you working at home during the next three months?

   How important is it to do what the following think you should do?

	FOR	AGAINST	IMPORTANT	UNIMPORTANT
a. Your supervisor	1 2 3 4 5 6 7		1 2 3 4 5 6 7	
b. Your co-workers	1 2 3 4 5 6 7		1 2 3 4 5 6 7	
c. Your company	1 2 3 4 5 6 7		1 2 3 4 5 6 7	
d. Your spouse (if married)	1 2 3 4 5 6 7		1 2 3 4 5 6 7	

6. Why are these group for or against you working at home during the next three months? Are there other groups or people that your influence your decision to work at home?

7. Overall, to what degree are the people most important to you and your job, for or against you working at home during the next three months

   1   2   3   4   5   6   7
   FOR   AGAINST

8. Given your current work situation, what is the likelihood that you will be working at home during the next three months?

   1   2   3   4   5   6   7
   LIKELY   UNLIKELY

WORKING AT HOME QUESTIONNAIRE – SECTION III

The purpose of this section is to gather information on the amount of time you spend on certain tasks, the importance of those tasks to your job, and your perceptions about your performance.

1. In the last 3 months, how many hours per week, on the average, did you spend working on:

HOURS PER WEEK

	0	1-5	6-10	11-15	16-20	21-25	25+
a. Developing and/or maintaining acceptable standards for products/services/equipment.	0	1-5	6-10	11-15	16-20	21-25	25+
b. Applying knowledge to solve job related problems for timely corrective action.	0	1-5	6-10	11-15	16-20	21-25	25+
c. Preparing reports or other documents in written or pictoral form.	0	1-5	6-10	11-15	16-20	21-25	25+
d. Developing an effective documentation system and keeping accurate records.	0	1-5	6-10	11-15	16-20	21-25	25+
e. Planning for both short term and long range goal achievement.	0	1-5	6-10	11-15	16-20	21-25	25+
f. Estimating and monitoring expenses to achieve cost effectiveness.	0	1-5	6-10	11-15	16-20	21-25	25+
g. Allocating materials to optimize utilization of resources.	0	1-5	6-10	11-15	16-20	21-25	25+
h. Communicating to an individual or group of individuals.	0	1-5	6-10	11-15	16-20	21-25	25+
i. Negotiating and cooperating with others to accomplish optimal utilization of resources.	0	1-5	6-10	11-15	16-20	21-25	25+
j. Serving as the head of a team/unit responsible for a given project(s).	0	1-5	6-10	11-15	16-20	21-25	25+
k. Keeping up-to-date technically.	0	1-5	6-10	11-15	16-20	21-25	25+
l. Other activies? Please describe.	0	1-5	6-10	11-15	16-20	21-25	25+

2. In the matrix below, place an "I" in the box which represents how important you feel each of these tasks was to your overall job in the last 3 months.

	N/A	LOW		MEDIUM		HIGH	
a. Developing and/or maintaining acceptable standards for products/services/equipment.							
b. Applying knowledge to solve job related problems for timely corrective action.							
c. Preparing reports or other documents in written or pictoral form.							
d. Developing an effective documentation system and keeping accurate records.							
e. Planning for both short term and long range goal achievement.							
f. Estimating and monitoring expenses to achieve cost effectiveness.							
g. Allocating materials to optimize utilization of resources.							
h. Communicating to an individual or group of individuals.							
i. Negotiating and cooperating with others to accomplish optimal utilization of resources.							
j. Serving as the head of a team/unit responsible for a given project(s).							
k. Keeping up-to-date technically.							
l. Other activies? (That you listed above)							

3. In the above matrix, place an "E" in the box which represents your perception of your effectiveness in doing each of the tasks in the last 3 months.

4. Please check the box indicating how well you feel your overall performance rated against your expectations during the last 3 months.

NOT ACCEPT-ABLE	PARTIALLY ACHIEVING EXPECTATIONS	ACHIEVING EXPECTATIONS	EXCEEDING EXPECTATIONS

5. During the last 3 months, what percent of time did you spend working alone on activities? _____ %

6. During the last 3 months, how many hours per week did you spend working at home:

				HOURS PER WEEK			
		0	1-5	6-10	11-15	16-20	21-25	25+

a. During regular work hours? ... 0   1-5   6-10   11-15   16-20   21-25   25+
b. Not during regular work hours? ... 0   1-5   6-10   11-15   16-20   21-25   25+

THANK YOU FOR YOUR TIME AND PATIENCE!

Appendix B

Descriptive Statistics, ANCOVA Results, and Graphical Analysis of Outcome Variables

Table B.1.   Analysis of Variance of the Demographic Variables

| Demographic Variables: | GROUP MEANS | | MEAN SQUARE ERROR | | F-SCORE | SIGNI- |
	CONTROL	TREATMENT	BETWEEN	WITHIN	VALUE	FICANCE
Age	34.5710	32.0630	47.0006	40.0845	1.1750	0.2880
Sex (0-female, 1-male)	0.0286	0.3750	0.0595	0.2360	0.2523	0.6190
No. years in organization	3.2140	3.0000	0.3429	7.0128	0.0489	0.8270
No. years in current position	2.5710	2.0000	2.4381	4.6224	0.5274	0.4740
Education	3.3570	3.9380	2.5149	2.4340	1.0332	0.3180
No. of people in household	2.0710	2.0000	0.0381	2.8189	0.0135	0.9080
Age of children in household	1.0000	0.7500	0.4667	1.2500	0.3733	0.5460
Commuting distance to work	13.2140	13.2500	0.0095	86.1199	0.0001	0.9920

Table B.2.   Analysis of Variance Treatment Breakdown of Demographic Variables

| Demographic Variables: | GROUP MEANS | | | MEAN SQUARE ERROR | | F-SCORE | SIGNI- |
	FULLTIME	PART-TIME	UNABLE	BETWEEN	WITHIN	VALUE	FICANCE
Age	31.6670	31.0000	34.2500	24.6183	42.1351	0.5843	0.6307
Sex (0-female, 1-male)	0.1670	0.6670	0.2500	0.2976	0.2221	1.3402	0.2829
No. years in organization	2.5000	3.3330	3.2500	0.9198	7.4592	0.1233	0.9455
No. years in current position	2.1670	1.8330	2.0000	0.9238	4.9652	0.1861	0.9049
Education	3.0000	4.6670	4.2500	3.7897	2.2807	1.6616	0.1997
No. of persons in household	3.5000	1.1670	1.0000	7.2349	2.2024	3.2850	0.0366
Age of children in household	1.1670	0.1670	1.0000	1.2667	1.2179	1.0400	0.3914
Commuting distance to work	14.6670	15.8330	7.2500	65.3643	85.2028	0.7672	0.5228

Table B.3.   Analysis of Covariance Results from the Working at Home Questionnaire Section on Communication

	TREATMENT EFFECT	COVARIATE EFFECT	TIME EFFECT	TIME x GROUP
General Communication:				
1.11 Time communicating face-to-face	0.09	1.68	0.40	0.04
1.12 Time communicating outside work group	0.85	11.04 **	0.07	0.27
1.13 Amount of conflicting communication	0.01	31.82 **	0.71	0.02
Horizontal Communication:				
1.21 Communication on job related subjects	0.72	1.86	2.30	0.00
1.22 Communication on non-job related subjects	0.03	36.38 **	1.69	0.31
Upward Communication:				
1.31 Communication with boss on performance	0.23	0.12	0.34	1.83
1.32 Communication with boss about yourself	0.13	0.00	0.14	1.30
1.33 Communication with boss about others	0.56	0.04	0.23	2.08
1.34 Communication with boss about organization	0.53	1.28	1.21	6.57 **
1.35 Communication with boss about tasks	0.04	10.83 **	0.07	1.65
Downward Communication:				
1.41 Communicating instructions to subordinates	0.10	8.60 **	1.52	0.38
1.42 Communicating job rationale to subordinates	0.00	5.69 *	0.13	1.17
1.43 Communicating org. proc. to subordinates	0.10	5.35 *	0.04	2.14
1.44 Giving feedback on perf. to subordinates	0.16	6.14 *	0.04	3.12
1.45 Communicating group goals to subordinates	0.01	13.23 **	2.74	0.00

Table B.4. Analysis of Covariance Breakdown of Treatment Results from the
Working at Home Questionnaire Section on Communication

	TREATMENT EFFECT	COVARIATE EFFECT	TIME EFFECT	TIME x GROUP
General Communication:				
1.11 Time communicating face-to-face	12.40 **	7.37 *	0.21	0.07
1.12 Time communicating outside work group	2.77	9.78 **	0.06	3.23 *
1.13 Amount of conflicting communication	0.92	31.44 **	0.19	1.65
Horizontal Communication:				
1.21 Communication on job related subjects	2.91	3.41 *	1.35	1.05
1.22 Communication on non-job related subjects	2.42	40.73 **	2.35	2.33
Upward Communication:				
1.31 Communication with boss on performance	2.60	0.08	1.23	1.46
1.32 Communication with boss about yourself	3.73 *	0.55	0.00	1.13
1.33 Communication with boss about others	2.07	0.71	0.06	0.85
1.34 Communication with boss about organization	3.44 *	4.19	4.19	3.68 *
1.35 Communication with boss about tasks	6.40 **	21.25 **	0.03	5.35 **
Downward Communication:				
1.41 Communicating instructions to subordinates	4.18 *	13.60 **	0.54	0.22
1.42 Communicating job rationale to subordinates	2.68	8.82 **	0.00	0.49
1.43 Communicating org. proc. to subordinates	1.77	5.48 *	0.08	1.07
1.44 Giving feedback on perf. to subordinates	3.19 *	9.71 **	0.50	2.03
1.45 Communicating group goals to subordinates	0.73	12.10 **	1.63	0.66

Figure B.1.   Amount of Time during Work Spent Communicating Face-to-Face

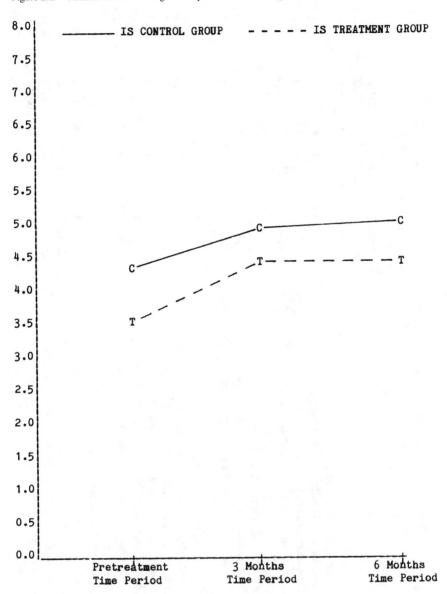

Fig. B.1 (contd.)

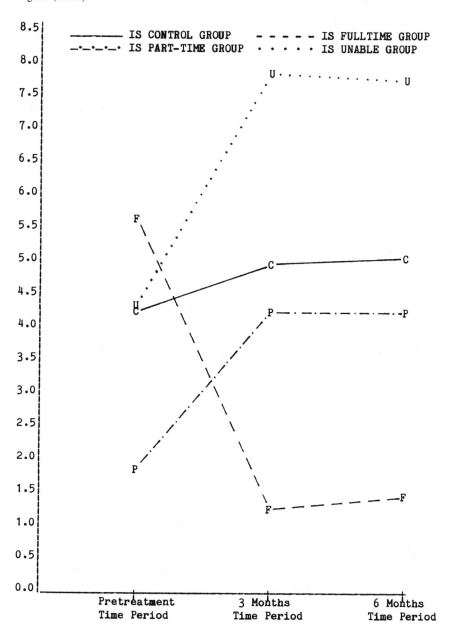

Figure B.2.   Communication with Group Members on Job Related Subjects

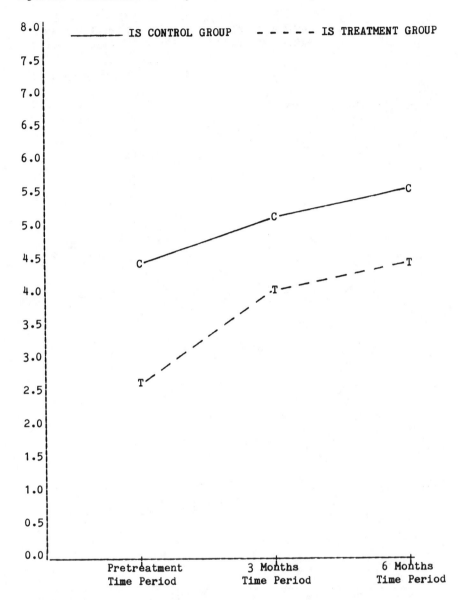

Fig. B.2 (contd.)

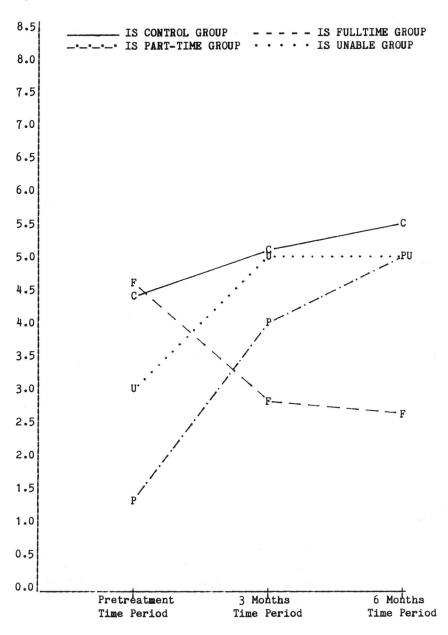

Figure B.3. Communication with Supervisor about What Tasks Need to Be Done

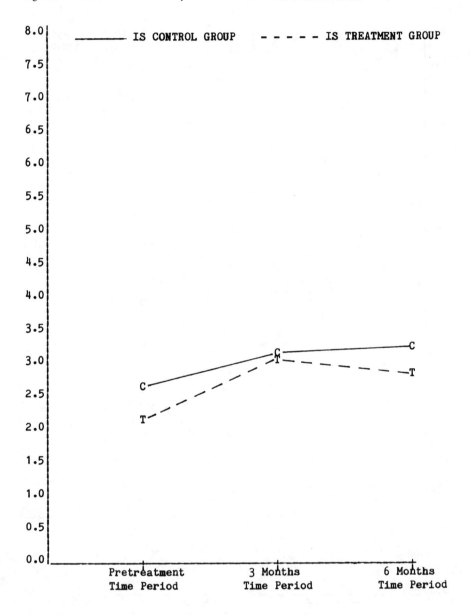

Fig. B.3 (contd.)

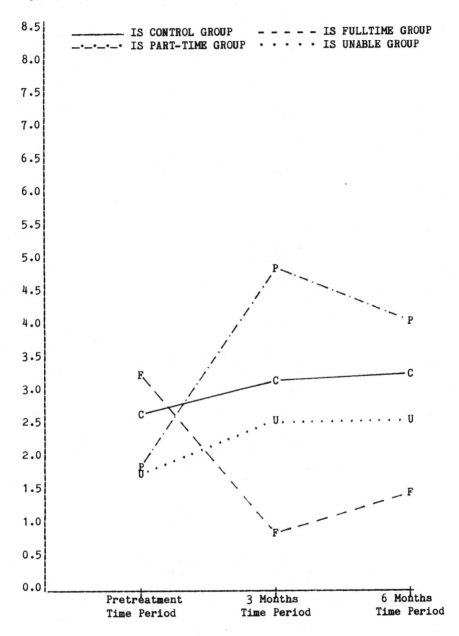

Figure B.4. Communicating Task or Job Instruction to Subordinates

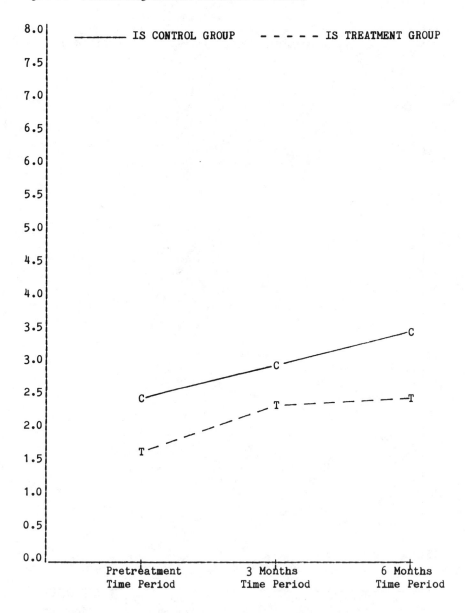

Fig. B.4 (contd.)

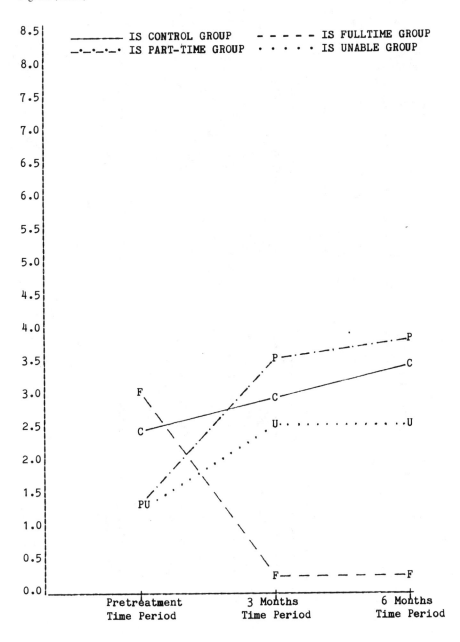

Table B.5.   Analysis of Covariance Results from the Working at Home
Questionnaire Section on Spatial-Physical Distance and Task

	TREATMENT EFFECT	COVARIATE EFFECT	TIME EFFECT	TIME x GROUP
Spatial-Physical Distance:				
2.11 Time spent away from work group	1.13	2.95	2.87	1.28
2.12 Time unable to talk due to distance	0.42	0.55	3.09	0.23
2.13 Time unable to ask questions	0.38	14.94 **	2.43	1.37
2.14 Time that no one was around for talk	0.43	2.29	0.45	0.05
2.15 Time unable to get at references	2.81	1.36	1.96	0.44
Work Flows:				
3.11 Time that was dependent on others	7.25 **	6.08 *	0.72	0.32
3.12 Time unable to work	7.97 **	5.36 *	0.69	0.08
Task Complexity:				
4.11 Time that job was unpredictable	1.49	0.67	0.03	3.44
4.12 Time when help was unavailable	0.01	16.00 **	2.48	1.26

Table B.6.   Analysis of Covariance Breakdown of Treatment Results from the
Working at Home Questionnaire Section on Spatial-Physical
Distance and Task

	TREATMENT EFFECT	COVARIATE EFFECT	TIME EFFECT	TIME x GROUP
Spatial-Physical Distance:				
2.11 Time spent away from work group	6.14 **	12.39 **	3.44	3.92 *
2.12 Time unable to talk due to distance	2.29	2.38	2.18	2.43
2.13 Time unable to ask questions	2.29	8.36	5.03 *	1.78
2.14 Time that no one was around for talk	0.24	2.29	1.24	2.48
2.15 Time unable to get at references	3.59 *	1.16	1.79	1.25
Work Flows:				
3.11 Time that was dependent on others	2.85 *	4.98 *	0.60	0.44
3.12 Time unable to work	2.13	5.56 *	0.33	2.11
Task Complexity:				
4.11 Time that job was unpredictable	0.71	0.42	1.02	1.68
4.12 Time when help was unavailable	0.76	17.31 **	1.88	0.56

Figure B.5.   Amount of Time that Was Spent Away from Members of Work Group

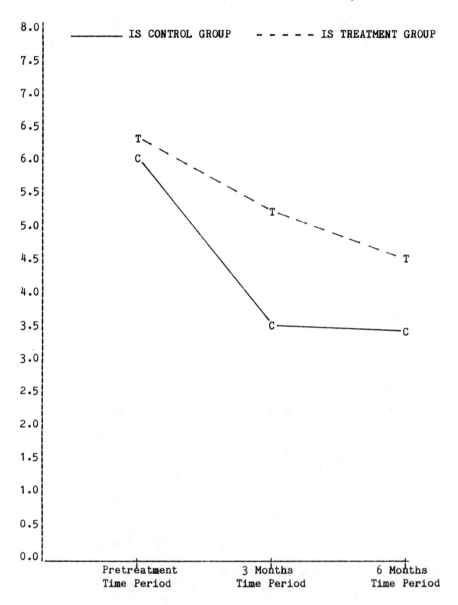

Fig. B.5 (contd.)

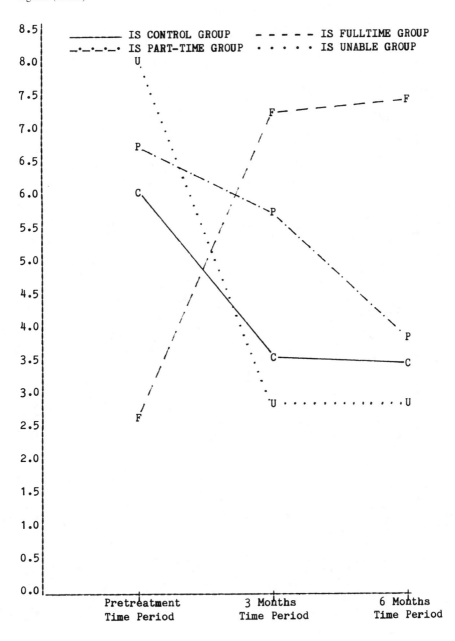

Figure B.6.   Time Unable to Have Face-to-Face Conversation When Needed

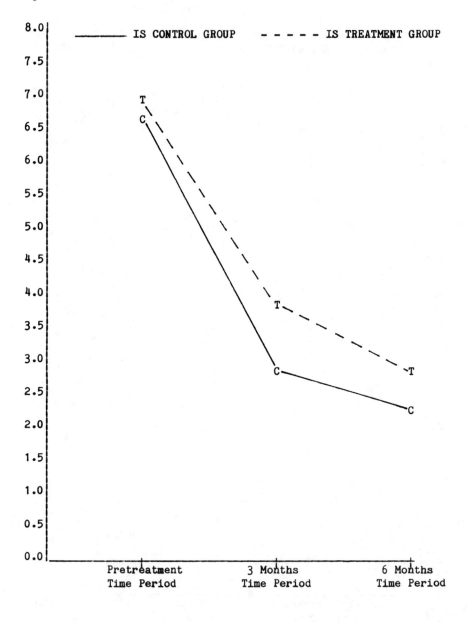

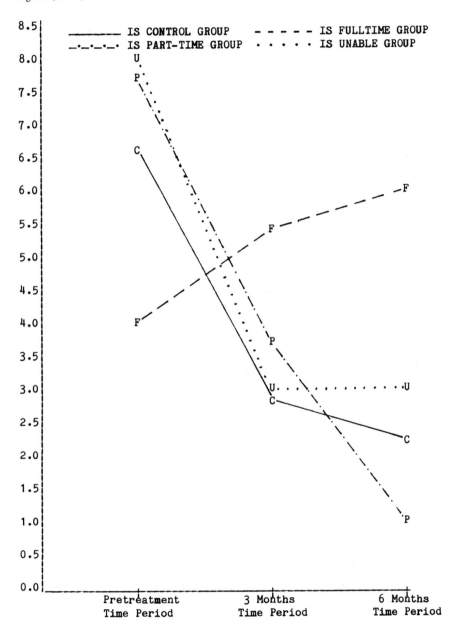

Figure B.7.   Time When Unable to Get Reference or Resource Material When Needed

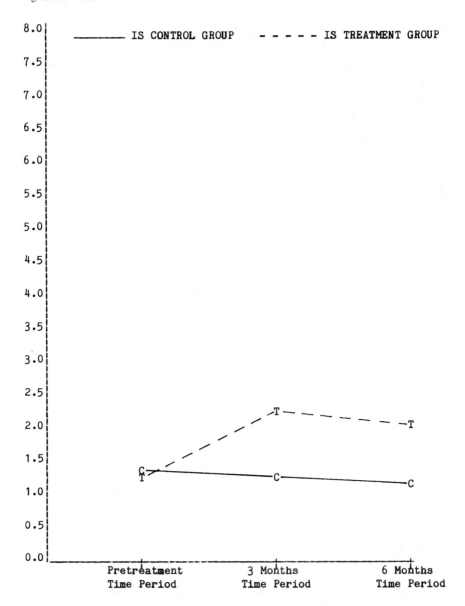

Fig. B.7 (contd.)

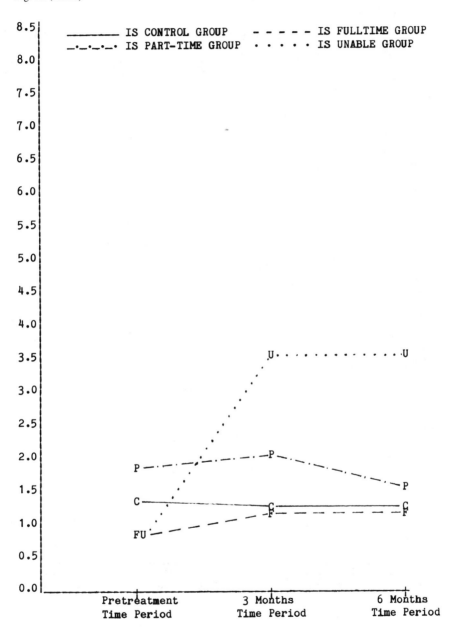

Figure B.8.   Amount of Time that Was Dependent upon Other Members of Work Group

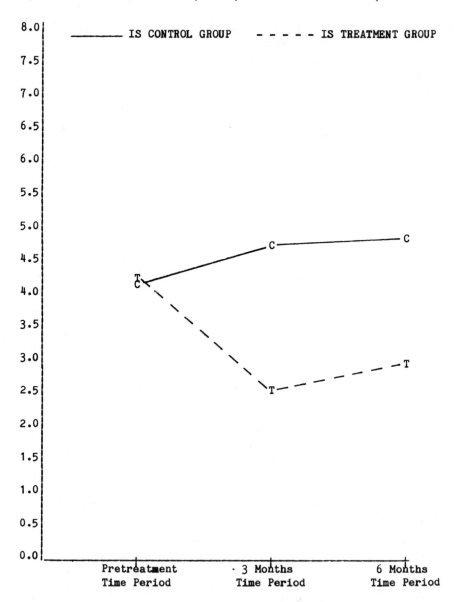

Fig. B.8 (contd.)

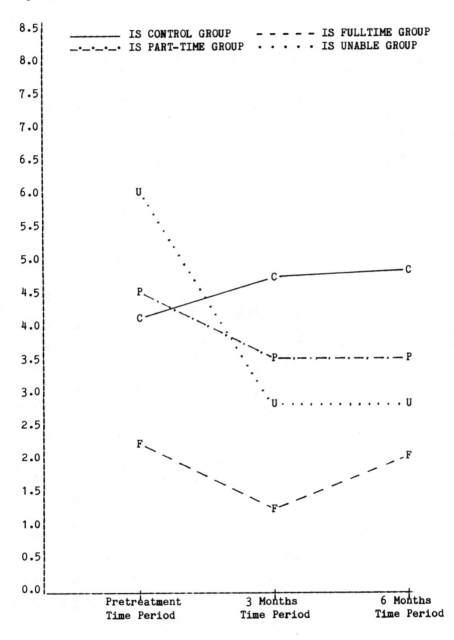

Table B7. Analysis of Covariance Results from the Working at Home Questionnaire Section on Organizational Behavior

	TREATMENT EFFECT	COVARIATE EFFECT	TIME EFFECT	TIME x GROUP
Feelings about the Job:				
5.11 Extent of commitment to work	0.12	3.24	3.16	0.35
5.12 Extent of working by a work standard	1.86	7.11 **	0.65	0.65
5.13 Extent of automatically increase work time	1.99	70.82 **	4.91	3.82 *
5.14 Extent of improving work methods	0.95	10.85 **	3.24	1.00
5.15 Extent of developing skills and abilities	0.52	14.33 **	0.01	0.01
5.16 Extent of feeling contented on job	0.09	2.50	4.20 *	6.57 *
5.17 Extent of sense of achievement on job	0.27	25.85 **	3.46 *	3.46 **
5.18 Extent of actually working while on the job	0.08	6.44 *	1.02	0.40
5.19 Extent of thought of quitting or transferring	0.93	2.68	2.92	2.92
Feelings about Peers and Co-workers:				
5.21 Degree of confidence & trust in work group	0.00	43.45 **	0.09	0.38
5.22 Degree that team members volunteered to help	0.01	1.25	0.32	0.32
5.23 Degree of identification with work group	2.54	34.93 **	0.21	0.02
Feelings about the Supervisor:				
5.31 Degree of boss's confidence & trust	0.13	37.18 **	0.18	1.63
5.32 Degree of confidence & trust in boss	2.21	32.52 **	0.44	1.96
5.33 Degree of providing complete & accurate info.	0.03	81.80 **	0.08	0.08
5.34 Degree necessary to distort reported info.	0.65	4.68 *	0.42	1.68
5.35 Degree that job problems were given to boss	0.55	28.86 **	0.02	0.02
5.36 Degree that human problems were given to boss	0.00	19.58 **	0.13	0.15
5.37 Degree of identification with boss's team	0.49	23.63 **	1.88	0.12
5.38 Degree of implementing boss's decisions	1.57	14.71 **	0.00	0.75

Table B.8.   Analysis of Covariance Breakdown of Treatment Results from the
Working at Home Questionnaire Section on Organizational Behavior

	TREATMENT EFFECT	COVARIATE EFFECT	TIME EFFECT	TIME x GROUP
Feelings about the Job:				
5.11 Extent of commitment to work	0.58	3.26	0.50	2.18
5.12 Extent of working by a work standard	1.12	4.66 *	0.76	0.83
5.13 Automatically increase work time	1.63	64.08 **	8.32 **	3.11 *
5.14 Extent of improving work methods	0.46	10.99 **	4.31 *	1.03
5.15 Developing skills and abilities	0.33	13.17 **	0.47	0.19
5.16 Extent of feeling contented on job	1.41	2.48	7.00 **	3.89 *
5.17 Sense of achievement on job	1.06	21.82 **	6.34 *	4.08 **
5.18 Actually working while on the job	0.21	5.60 *	1.64	0.48
5.19 Thinking of transfer or quitting	0.45	3.78	2.32	0.94
Feelings about Peers and Co-workers:				
5.21 Degree of confidence & trust	1.69	43.93 **	0.30	1.60
5.22 Help volunteered by team members	0.77	1.46	0.32	1.26
5.23 Identification with work group	3.34 *	36.46 **	0.20	1.08
Feelings about the Supervisor:				
5.31 Degree of boss's confidence & trust	0.88	20.12 **	0.10	0.36
5.32 Degree of confidence & trust in boss	0.73	28.78 **	2.68	2.80
5.33 Providing complete & accurate info.	1.00	87.63 **	0.00	0.32
5.34 Distorting reported information	0.66	5.86 *	0.01	0.64
5.35 Providing boss with job problems	0.68	22.71 **	0.18	0.39
5.36 Providing boss with human problems	0.76	14.76 **	0.30	0.25
5.37 Identification with boss's team	0.59	17.65 **	0.99	0.15
5.38 Implementing boss's decisions	3.67 *	19.71 **	0.15	0.42

Figure B.9.   Extent to which Work Pace Was Increased and Work Breaks Shortened

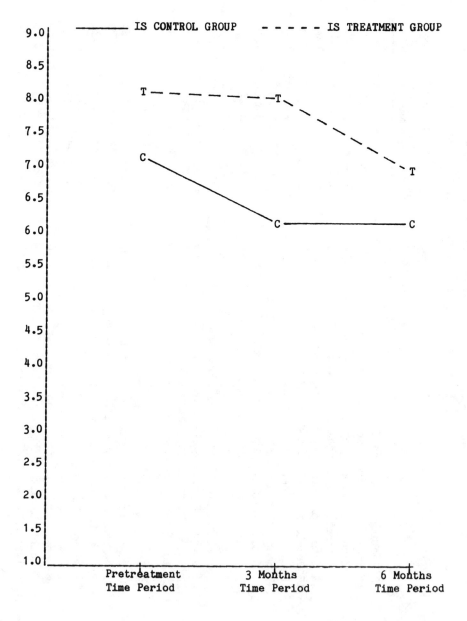

Fig. B.9 (contd.)

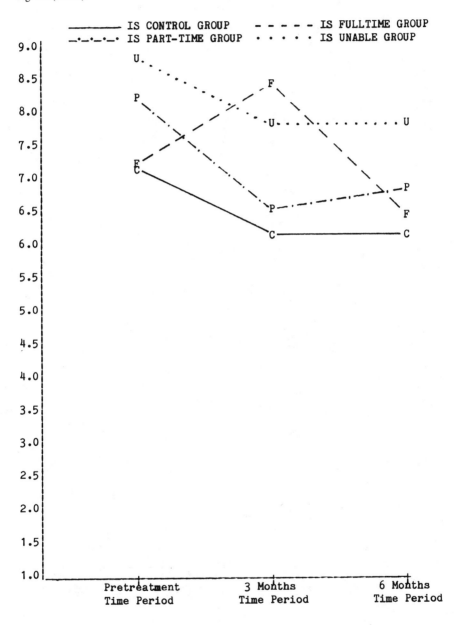

Figure B.10.   Extent of Trying to Improve Work Methods to Solve Work Problems

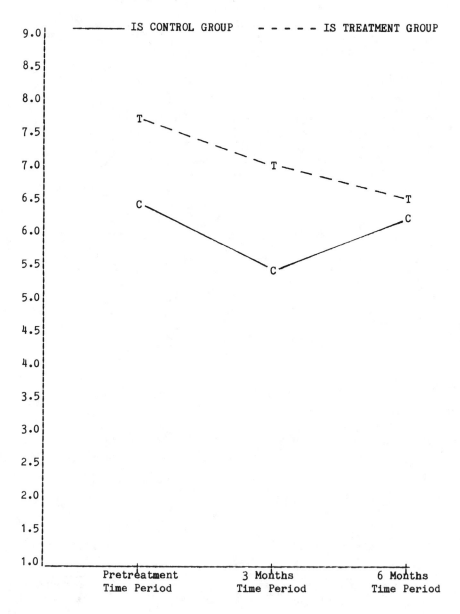

Fig. B.10 (contd.)

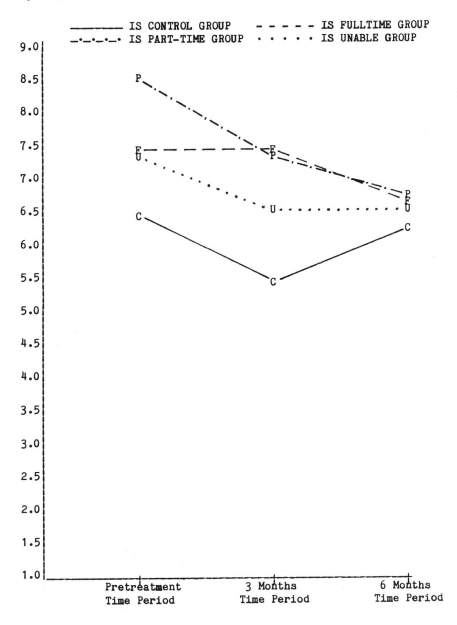

Figure B.11. Extent of Feeling Contented Rather than Frustrated in Doing Job

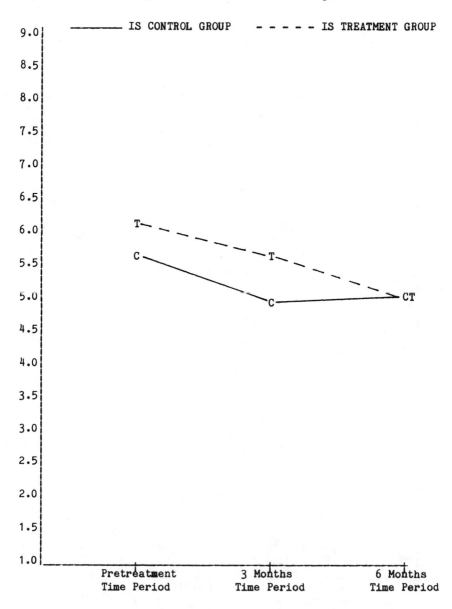

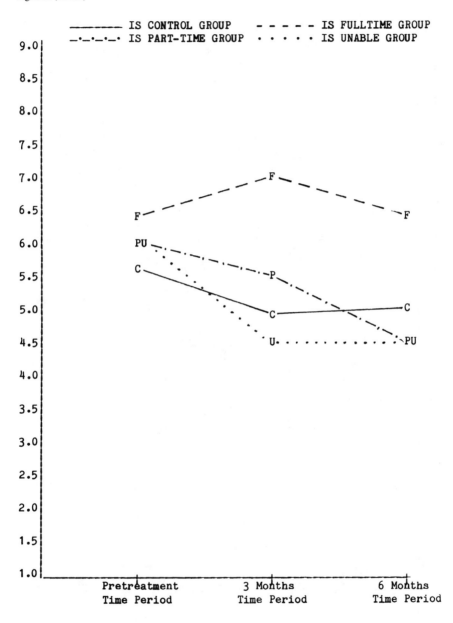

Figure B.12.   Extent of Having a Sense of Achievement in Performing the Job

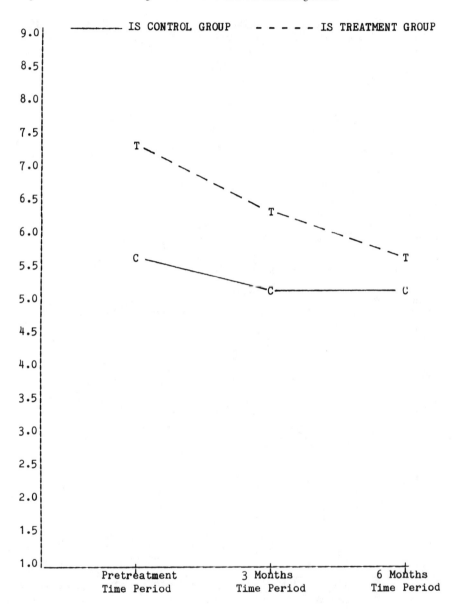

Fig. B.12 (contd.)

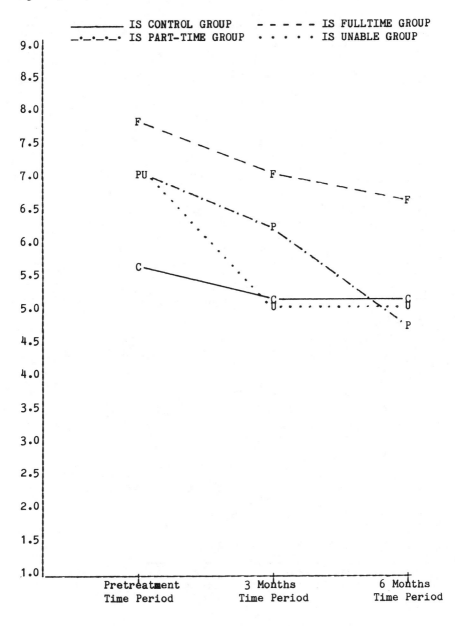

Figure B.13. Degree of Identification with Work Group

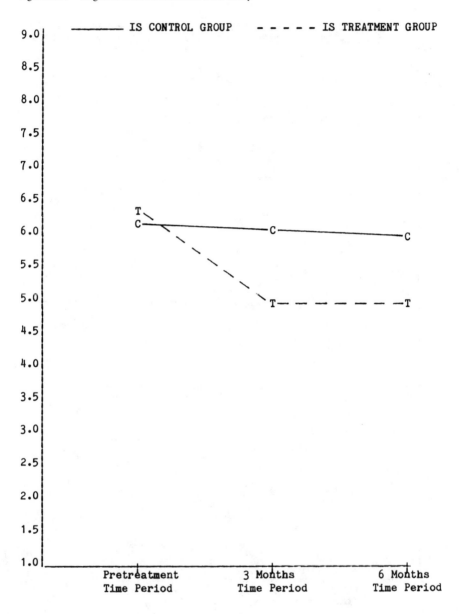

Fig. B.13 (contd.)

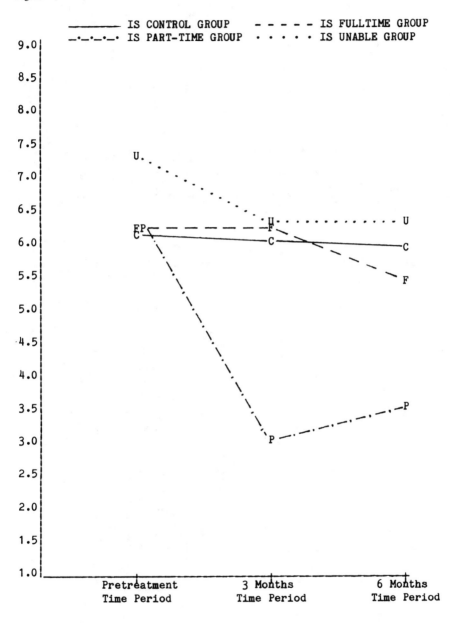

Table B.9.   Analysis of Covariance Results from the Minnesota Satisfaction Questionnaire

		TREATMENT EFFECT	COVARIATE EFFECT	TIME EFFECT	TIME x GROUP
1	Ability to serve other people	0.94	59.74 **	1.26	0.65
2	Ability to try own ideas	1.01	59.00 **	0.09	1.78
3	Job is not morally wrong	0.20	19.26 **	0.12	0.12
4	Ability to work alone on job	1.02	8.01 **	0.71	0.33
5	Amount of variety in job	1.36	16.28 **	0.00	2.22
6	Ability to direct actions of others	0.27	38.77 **	0.02	1.41
7	Ability to do best liked work	0.03	33.37 **	1.70	5.81 *
8	Social position that job provides	0.48	32.65 **	0.03	0.88
9	Company policies and practices	0.10	60.00 **	0.50	3.99 *
10	Supervisor relations	0.88	24.56 **	0.77	0.77
11	Job security	1.46	12.73 **	3.16	0.87
12	Job pay	1.82	21.12 **	1.72	0.24
13	Office working conditions	5.85 *	9.91 **	4.03	4.03
14	Opportunities for advancement	1.51	4.90 *	4.23 *	5.12 *
15	Technical "know how" of supervisor	0.35	21.27 **	2.01	2.01
16	Relations with co-workers	0.39	25.90 **	0.31	0.13
17	Ability to plan work	0.13	18.70 **	0.30	1.18
18	Feedback on job performance	0.53	17.85 **	1.22	2.10
19	Ability to see results of work	0.01	36.99 **	0.43	0.93
20	Ability to be active during work	0.21	26.31 **	0.85	2.15
	TOTAL OVERALL JOB SATISFACTION	0.11	38.16 **	1.54	3.98 *

Table B.10. Analysis of Covariance Breakdown of Treatment Results from the Minnesota Satisfaction Questionnaire

	TREATMENT EFFECT	COVARIATE EFFECT	TIME EFFECT	TIME x GROUP
1 Ability to serve other people	1.16	62.71 **	1.92	3.30 *
2 Ability to try own ideas	0.56	54.68 **	0.54	0.92
3 Job is not morally wrong	0.83	17.83 **	0.03	1.56
4 Ability to work alone on job	3.44 *	6.49 **	0.79	0.27
5 Amount of variety in job	3.17 *	15.23 **	0.34	0.87
6 Ability to direct actions of others	3.15 *	31.13 **	0.11	2.00
7 Ability to do best liked work	0.22	31.47 **	4.28 *	3.53 *
8 Social position that job provides	0.58	32.27 **	0.28	1.99
9 Company policies and practices	1.11	57.81 **	1.84	2.26 *
10 Supervisor relations	2.48	27.52 **	1.08	0.60
11 Job security	3.54 *	17.08 **	4.48 *	4.26 *
12 Job pay	1.22	18.69 **	1.68	1.08
13 Office working conditions	4.57 **	9.76 **	6.90 **	3.91 *
14 Opportunities for advancement	1.45	4.76 *	8.44 **	5.58 **
15 Technical "know how" of supervisor	0.49	17.55 **	4.44 *	6.55 **
16 Relations with co-workers	0.76	23.67 **	0.10	0.05
17 Ability to plan work	0.39	17.00 **	0.00	1.03
18 Feedback on job performance	0.21	16.56 **	2.24	1.82
19 Ability to see results of work	1.96	43.17 **	0.79	0.51
20 Ability to be active during work	0.30	25.19 **	2.36	5.06 **
TOTAL OVERALL JOB SATISFACTION	0.91	37.51 **	3.92 *	4.64 **

Figure B.14.   Job Satisfaction Concerning Office Working Conditions

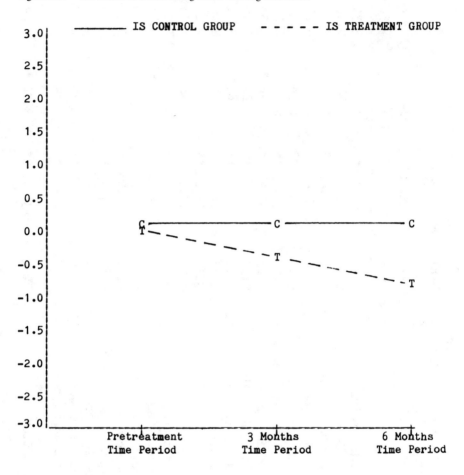

Fig. B.14 (contd.)

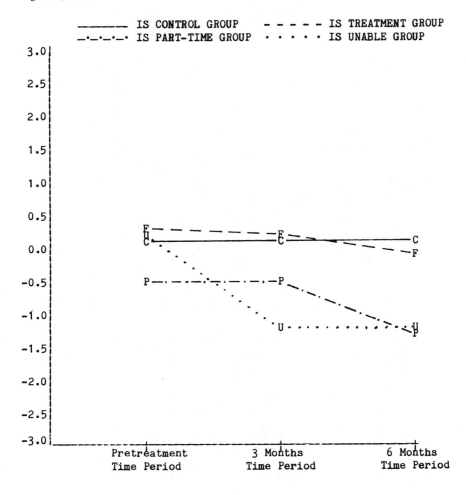

Table B.11.   Analysis of Covariance Results from the Working at Home
Questionnaire Section on the Use of Technology

	TREATMENT EFFECT	COVARIATE EFFECT	TIME EFFECT	TIME x GROUP
Use of the Telephone:				
6.11 Amount of group member communication by phone	10.29 **	9.96 **	0.03	0.29
6.12 Amount of supervisor communication by phone	9.69 **	0.62	0.63	0.00
6.13 Amount of subordinate communication by phone	3.93 *	20.70 **	3.55	1.09
6.14 Amount of user communication by phone	7.42 **	10.12 **	2.00	0.00
6.15 Extent of work that was dependent on the phone	9.02 **	9.24 **	0.00	0.14
Use of the Terminal or Computer:				
6.21 Amt. of group member communication by computer	2.07	4.76 *	0.26	0.09
6.22 Amt. of supervisor communication by computer	0.18	6.60 **	1.26	0.14
6.23 Amt. of subordinate communication by computer	2.24	7.92 **	0.51	0.51
6.24 Amt. of user communication by computer	0.45	3.50	0.00	0.63
6.25 Extent of work dependent upon using a computer	1.68	11.71 **	0.04	0.04

Table B.12.   Analysis of Covariance Breakdown of Treatment Results from the
Working at Home Questionnaire Section on the Use of Technology

	TREATMENT EFFECT	COVARIATE EFFECT	TIME EFFECT	TIME x GROUP
Use of the Telephone:				
6.11 Amount of group member communication by phone	9.36 **	16.71 **	0.01	0.37
6.12 Amount of supervisor communication by phone	6.50 **	0.54	0.10	0.85
6.13 Amount of subordinate communication by phone	1.20	17.20 **	3.77 *	2.85
6.14 Amount of user communication by phone	3.51 *	8.68 **	0.41	0.14
6.15 Extent of work that was dependent on the phone	9.85 **	15.01 **	0.01	0.08
Use of the Terminal or Computer:				
6.21 Amt. of group member communication by computer	1.23	4.50 *	0.82	2.83
6.22 Amt. of supervisor communication by computer	0.43	4.33 *	2.12	0.58
6.23 Amt. of subordinate communication by computer	2.90 *	7.26 **	0.10	0.17
6.24 Amt. of user communication by computer	0.86	4.15 *	0.19	1.74
6.25 Extent of work dependent upon using a computer	4.41 **	11.59 **	0.00	0.53

Figure B.15. How Much Communication with Other Group Members Was By Phone

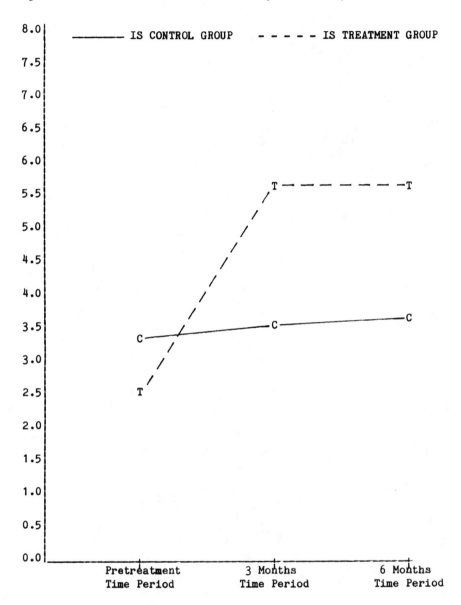

Fig. B.15 (contd.)

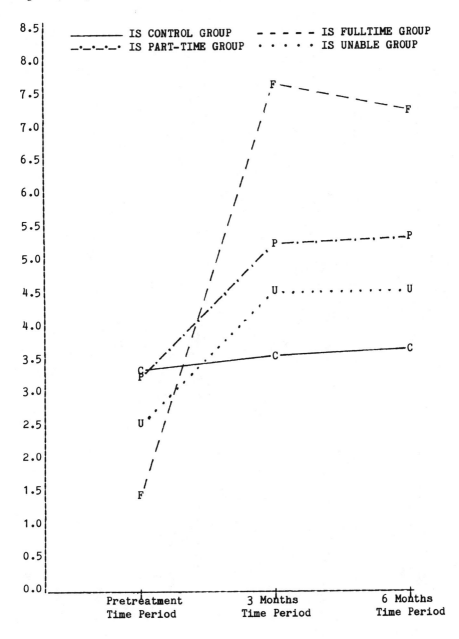

Figure B.16.   How Much Communication with Supervisor Was By Phone

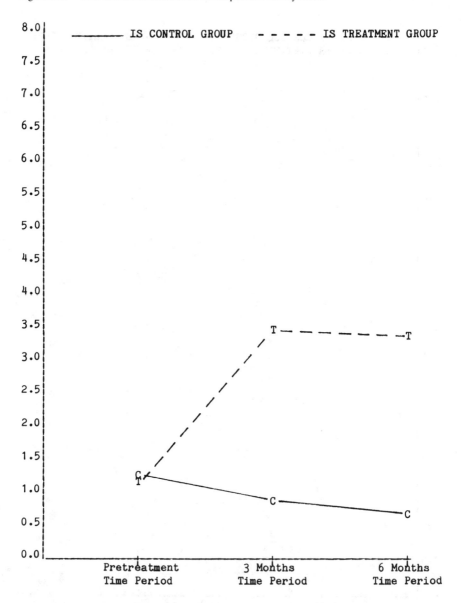

Fig. B.16 (contd.)

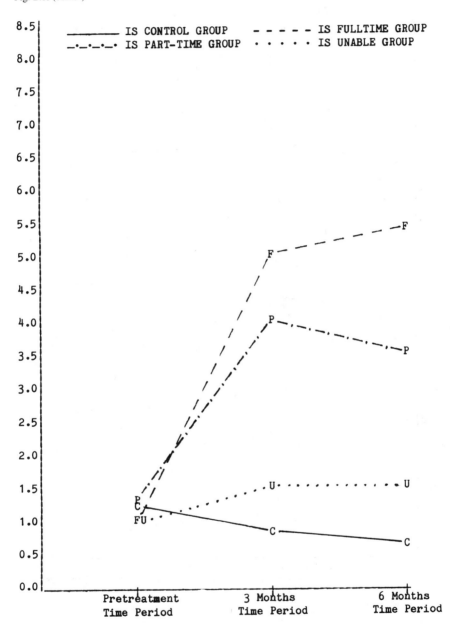

Figure B.17.   Extent of Work that Was Dependent on Using the Phone

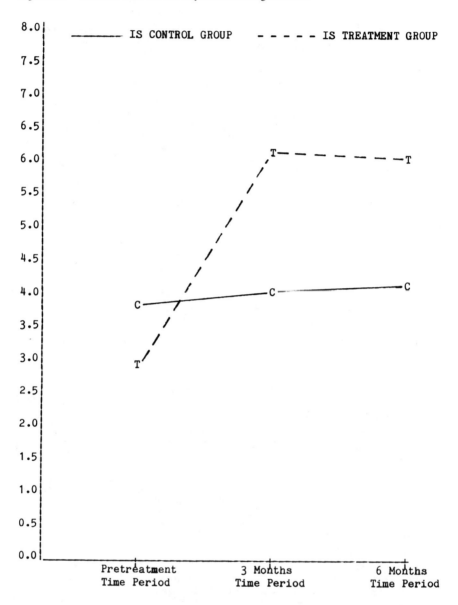

Fig. B.17 (contd.)

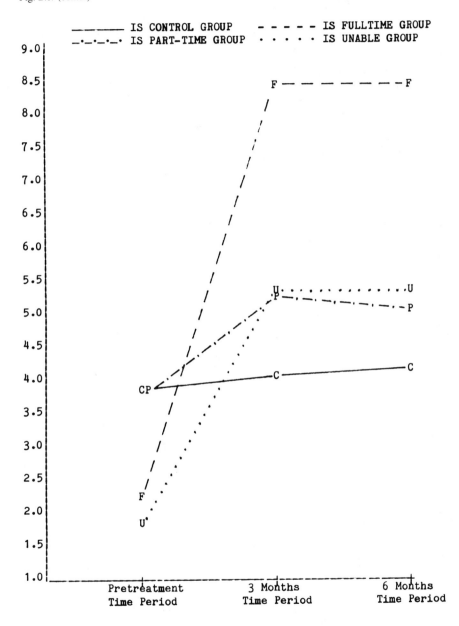

Figure B.18.   How Much Communication with Other Group Members Was By Computer

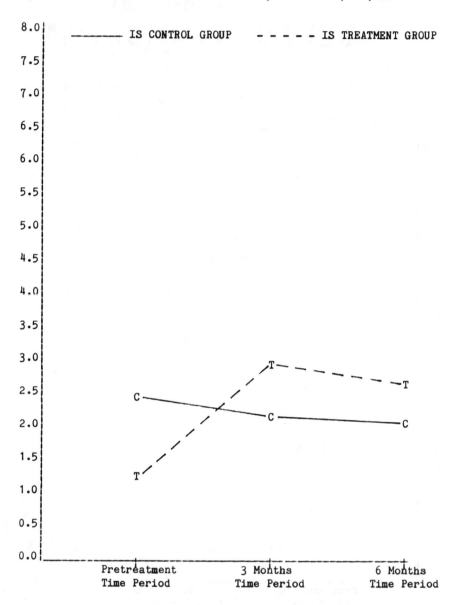

Fig. B.18 (contd.)

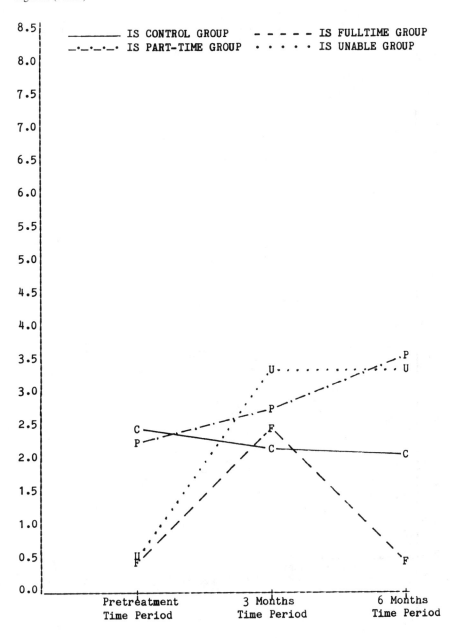

Figure B.19.   How Much Communication with People Who Work for You Was By Computer

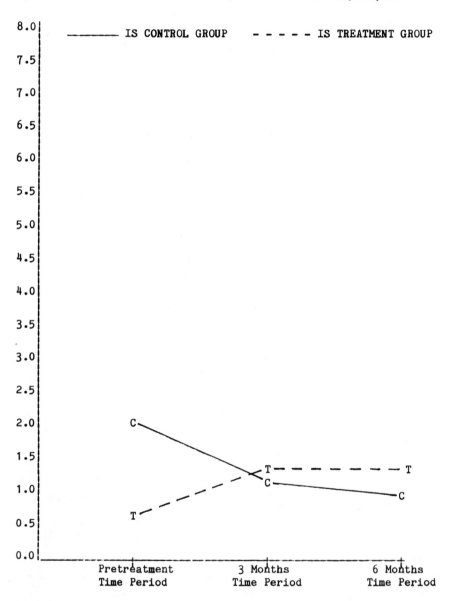

Fig. B.19 (contd.)

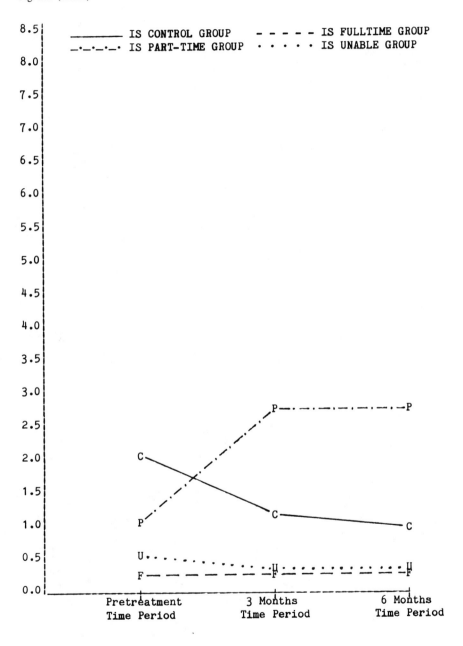

Figure B.20.   Extent of Work that Was Dependent on Using the Computer

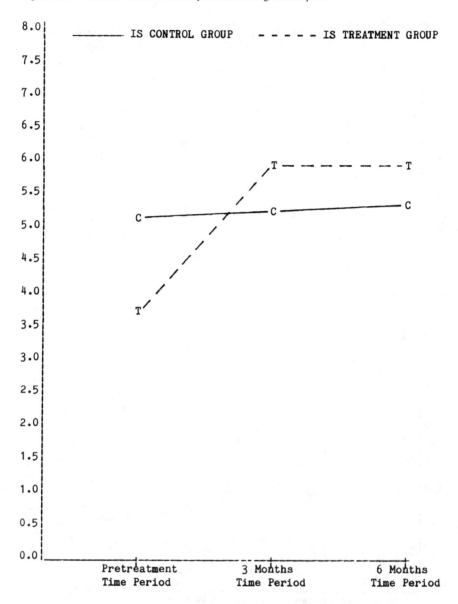

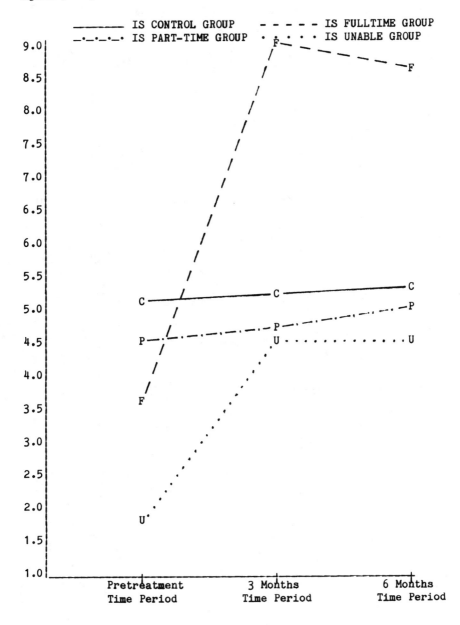

Notes

Chapter 1

1. Alvin Toffler, *The Third Wave* (New York: William Morrow and Company, Inc., 1980), p. 210.

2. Ibid., p. 210.

3. David Bell, "Communications Technology — For Better or For Worse," *Harvard Business Review*, May-June 1979, p. 21.

4. M. U. Porat, *The Information Economy: Definition and Measurement* (Washington, D.C.: U.S. Department of Commerce, 1977), p. 1.

5. Toffler, *The Third Wave*, p. 215.

6. "If Home Is Where the Worker Is," *Business Week*, May 3, 1982, p. 66.

7. R. A. Manning et al., "Alternative Work Site Programs," Control Data Corporation report presented to the Office Technology Research Group, October 1981, p. 11.

8. Dorothy Kunkin Heller, "More Corporations Endorse Telecommuting for Data Processors," *Infoworld*, December 14, 1981, p. 18.

9. Toffler, *The Third Wave*, p. 213.

10. Dr. Even Peele, "How to Make Telecommuting Work," *Personal Computing*, May 1982, p. 38.

11. Kenneth L. Kraemer, "Telecommunications-Transportation Substitution and Energy Productivity: A Re-Examination," University of California, Irvine: Public Policy Research Organization, June 1981, p. 38.

12. James Martin, *Telematic Society — A Challenge for Tomorrow* (New Jersey: Prentice-Hall, Inc., 1981), p. 127.

Chapter 2

1. "Office Work in the Home: Scenarios and Prospects for the '80s," *Diabold Report*, Fall 1981, p. 5.

2. Ibid., p. 1.

3. Steven Stibbens, "People: The Cost of Finding, Hiring and Training," *Infosystems*, January 1981, p. 46.

4. "Office Work in the Home," *Diabold Report*, p. 1.

5. Alvin Toffler, *The Third Wave* (New York: William Morrow and Company, Inc., 1980), p. 219.

6. "Office Work in the Home," *Diabold Report*, p. 1.

7. Toffler, *The Third Wave*, pp. 211-12.

8. H. J. Leavitt, "Applied Organizational Change in Industry: Structural, Technological and Humanistic Approaches," In: J. C. March (ed.), *Handbook of Organizations* (Chicago: Rand McNally, 1965), p. 1148.

9. Norman Macrae, "How to Survive in the Age of Telecommuting," *Management Review*, November 1978, p. 14.

10. "A Preamble to Change," *Personal Computing*, May 1982, p. 5.

11. "Office Work in the Home," *Diabold Report*, p. 6.

12. Toffler, *The Third Wave*, p. 215.

13. Kenneth L. Kraemer, "Telecommunications-Transportation Substitution and Energy Productivity: A Re-Examination," University of California, Irvine: Public Policy Research Organization, June 1981, p. 46.

14. Ibid., p. 47.

Chapter 3

1. "If Home Is Where the Worker Is," *Business Week*, May 3, 1982, p. 66.

2. Ray Vicker, "Computer Terminals Allow More People to Work at Home Instead of Commuting," *Wall Street Journal*, August 4, 1981, p. 48.

3. "On-line Homework a Prelude to New Job Status?" *Data Communications*, October 1980, p. 34.

4. [M. Grangeis], "The Potential for Telecommuting," *Business Week*, January 26, 1981, pp. 94-103.

5. "Can Telecommunications Replace Travel?," *EDP Analyzer*, 20, no. 4, April 1982, p. 2.

6. Tom Ewing, "Vermont Software House: A Home for 'Rural Technologists,'" *Software*, January 21, 1980.

7. Dorothy Kunkin Heller, "More Corporations Endorse Telecommuting for Data Processing," *Infoworld*, December 14, 1981, p. 18.

8. "Office Work in the Home: Scenarios and Prospects for the '80s," *Diabold Report*, Fall 1981, p. 13.

9. Ibid., p. 18.

10. Margo Downing-Faircloth, "Would Working at Home Be Wise?" *Personal Computing*, May 1982, pp. 42-46.

11. Heller, "Corporations Endorse Telecommuting," p. 25.

12. "Replace Travel?" *EDP Analyzer*, p. 12.

13. F. A. Dubiel, "Management Opinion," *Administrative Management*, p. 104.

14. "Replace Travel?" *EDP Analyzer*, p. 12.

15. [M. Grangeis], "The Potential," p. 98.

Chapter 4

1. "Office Work in the Home: Scenarios and Prospects for the '80s," *Diabold Report*, Fall 1981, p. i.

2. Ibid., p. 2.

3. Ibid., p. 9.

4. Dr. Even Peele, "How to Make Telecommuting Work," *Personal Computing*, May 1982, p. 38.

5. Kenneth L. Kracmer, "Telecommunications-Transportation Substitution and Energy Productivity: A Re-Examination," University of California, Irvine: Public Policy Research Organization, June 1981, pp. 39-40.

6. David A. Nadler and Michael L. Tushman, "A Model for Diagnosing Organizational Behavior," *Organizational Dynamics*, Autumn 1980, pp. 35-36.

7. Thomas S. Kuhn, *The Structure of Scientific Revolutions* (Chicago: The University of Chicago Press, 1970), p. 44.

8. H. J. Leavitt, "Applied Organizational Change in Industry: Structural, Technological, and Humanistic Approaches," In: J. C. March (ed.), *Handbook of Organizations* (Chicago: Rand McNally, 1965), p. 1145.

9. Ibid.

10. Peter G. W. Keen, "Information Systems and Organizational Change," *Communication of the ACM*, 24, no. 1, January 1981, p. 25.

11. Leavitt, "Applied Organizational Change in Industry," p. 1145.

12. Ibid.

13. H. Randolph Bobbitt, Jr., and Orlando C. Behling, "Organizational Behavior: A Review of the Literature," *Journal of Higher Education* 52, no. 1, 1981, p. 32.

14. Leavitt, "Applied Organizational Change in Industry," p. 1144.

15. Bobbitt, "Organizational Behavior," p. 34.

16. Leavitt, "Applied Organizational Change in Industry," p. 1146.

17. Ibid., p. 1145.

18. Jack M. Nilles et al., *The Telecommunication Transportation Tradeoff* (New York: John Wiley and Sons, 1977), p. 11.

19. Ibid.

20. Ibid., p. 12.

21. Ibid., p. 14.

22. Ibid., p. 15.

23. "Office Work in the Home," *Diabold Report*, p. 3.

24. R. Johansen, J. Vallee, and K. Spangler, *Electronic Meetings: Technical Alternatives and Social Choices*, (Reading, Mass.: Addison-Wesley Publishing Co., 1979), p. 104

25. F.A. Dubiel, "Management Opinion," *Administrative Management*, p. 104.

26. Leavitt, "Applied Organizational Change in Industry," p. 1148.

27. Paul Freiberger, "Telecommuting Makes Inroads," *Infoworld*, October 12, 1981, p. 13.

28. Dubiel, "Management Opinion," p. 104.

29. Margo Downing-Faircloth, "Would Working at Home Be Wise?" *Personal Computing*, May 1982, p. 42.

30. Leavitt, "Applied Organizational Change in Industry," p. 1144.

31. "Can Telecommunications Replace Travel?" *EDP Analyzer*, 20, no. 4 , April 1982, p. 11.

32. Nilles, *The Tradeoff*, p. 10.

33. "Replace Travel?" *EDP Analyzer*, p. 11

34. "Office Work in the Home," *Diabold Report*, p. 29.

35. Ibid.

36. Charles Handy, "The Changing Shape of Work," *Organizational Dynamics*, Autumn 1980, p. 31.

37. Johansen, *Electronic Meetings*, p. 133.

38. Ibid.

39. Bobbitt, "Organizational Behavior," p. 36.

40. Leavitt, "Applied Organizational Change in Industry," p. 1151.

41. R. C. Harkness, *Technology Assessment of Telecommunications/Transportation Interactions* (Menlo Park, California: Stanford Research Institute, 1977), p. 107.

42. "If Home Is Where the Worker Is," *Business Week*, May 3, 1982, p. 66.

43. Ray Vicker, "Computer Terminals Allow More People to Work at Home Instead of Commuting," *Wall Street Journal*, August 4, 1981, p. 49.

44. [M. Grangeis], "The Potential for Telecommuting," *Business Week*, January 26, 1981, p. 94.

45. Dorothy Kunkin Heller, "More Corporations Endorse Telecommuting for Data Processors," *Infoworld*, December 14, 1981, p. 18.

46. Ibid., p. 19.

47. Ibid.

48. "Office Work in the Home," *Diabold Report*, p. x.

49. Heller, "Corporations Endorse Telecommuting," p. 19.

50. Ibid.

51. Kathy Chin, "Home Is Where the Job Is," *Infoworld*, 6, no. 17, April 23, 1984, p. 36.

52. Leavitt, "Applied Organizational Change in Industry," p. 1144.

53. Bobbitt, "Organizational Behavior," p. 34.

54. Johansen, *Electronic Meetings*, p. 135.

55. Ronald P. Uhlig, "Human Factors in Computer Message Systems," *Datamation*, May 1977, pp. 121-26.

56. Nicole F. Leduc, "Communicating Through Computers," *Telecommunication Policy*, September 1979, p. 237.

57. Jacques Vallee et al., "Pragmatics and Dynamics of Computer Conferencing: A Summary of Findings from the Forum Project," *Proceedings of the Third International Conference on Computer Communications*, 1976, p. 210.

58. Leduc, "Communicating Through Computers," p. 243.

Chapter 5

1. Thomas D. Cook and Donald T. Campbell, *Quasi-Experimentation: Design and Analysis Issues for Field Settings* (Chicago: Rand McNally College Publishing Company, 1979), p. 4.

2. Ibid., pp. 5-6.

3. Ibid., pp. 7-8.

4. Ibid., p. 6.

5. Ibid., p. 7.

6. Ibid., p. 103.

7. Ibid., pp. 32-36.

Chapter 7

1. D. J. Weiss et al., *Minnesota Studies in Vocational Rehabilitation: 22, Manual for the Minnesota Satisfaction Questionnaire*. Vocational Psychology Research, University of Minnesota, 1967.

2. I. Ajzen and M. Fishbein, *Understanding Attitudes and Predicting Social Behavior* (New Jersey: Prentice-Hall, Inc., 1980).

3. D. J. Weiss et al., *Manual for the Minnesota Satisfaction Questionnaire*.

4. D. Katz and R.L. Kahn, *The Social Psychology of Organizations*, 2nd edition (New York: John Wiley & Sons, 1978), pp. 440-48.

5. A. J. Melcher, *Structure and Process of Organizations: A System Approach* (New Jersey: Prentice-Hall, Inc., 1976).

Chapter 8

1. John C. Flanagan, "The Critical Incident Technique," *Psychological Bulletin* 51, no. 4, July 1954.

2. Ibid., p. 327.

3. Ibid.

4. Thomas D. Cook and Donald T. Campbell, *Quasi-Experimentation: Design and Analysis Issues for Field Settings*, (Chicago: Rand McNally College Publishing Company, 1979), pp. 104-12.

5. Ibid., p. 106.

6. Ibid., p. 112.

7. Ibid., p. 153.

8. Ibid., p. 155.

9. W. J. Dixon and M. B. Brown (eds.), *BMDP-79: Biomedical Computer Programs, P-Series*, (Berkeley: University of California Press, 1979), p. 562.

10. Ibid., p. 570.

11. Cook, *Quasi-Experimentation*, pp. 159-70.

12. Ibid., p. 164.

Bibliography

ABA Banking Journal, "Chicago Bank Puts Terminals Into Employees' Homes to Do Work Formerly Done in the Office," pp. 72-74.

Alter, S., "Implementation Risk Analysis," Working Paper, University of Southern California, February 11, 1976.

Alter, S. and Ginzberg, M., "Managing Uncertainty in MIS Implementation," *Sloan Management Review*, Fall 1978, pp. 23-31.

Ajzen, I. and Fishbein, M., *Understanding Attitudes and Predicting Social Behavior* (New Jersey: Prentice-Hall, Inc., 1980).

Argyris, C., "The Individual and the Organization: An Empirical Test," *Administrative Science Quarterly* 4, no. 2, 1959, pp. 145-67.

———, *Understanding Organizational Behavior* (Homewood, Ill.: Dorsey Press, 1960).

Beere, M. P., "The Power of Telecommunications," *Computerworld Extra*, March 18, 1981, pp. 6-10.

Behling, O. C., "The Meaning of Dissatisfaction with Factory Work," *Management of Personnel Quarterly* 3, 1964, pp. 11-16.

Bell, D., "Communications Technology — For Better or For Worse," *Harvard Business Review,* May-June 1979.

Blood, M. R. and Hulin, C. L., "Alienation, Environmental Characteristics on Worker Responses," *Journal of Applied Psychology,* 1967, pp. 284-91.

Bobbitt, H., Jr. and Behling, O. C., "Organizational Behavior: A Review of the Literature," *Journal of Higher Education* 52, no. 1, 1981.

Bostrom, R. P. and Heinen, J. S., "MIS Problem and Failures: A Socio-Technical Perspective," MISRC Working Paper, WP-76-07, 1976, University of Minnesota, 1976.

———, "MIS Problems and Failures: A Socio-Technical Perspective: The Causes," *MIS Quarterly,* September 1977, pp. 17-32.

Brief, A. P. and Aldag, R. J., "Employee Reactions to Job Characteristics: A Constructive Replication," *Journal of Applied Psychology* 60, no. 2, 1975, pp. 182-86.

Bryan, J. F. and Locke, E. F., "Goal-Setting as a Means of Increasing Motivation," *Journal of Applied Psychology* 51, 1967, pp. 274-77.

Business Week, "If Home Is Where the Worker Is," May 3, 1982, p. 66.

Cascio, W. F., *Applied Psychology in Personnel Management,* Reston, Virginia: Reston Publishing Company, Inc., 1978.

Chin, K. "Home Is Where the Job Is," *Infoworld*, April 23, 1984, 6, no. 17, p. 36

Churchman, C. W. and Schainblatt, A. N., "The Researcher and the Manager: A Dialectic of Implementation," *Management Science*, February 1965, pp. B69-B87.

Control Data Corporation, interviews with professionals involved in Alternative Work Site Program, April 1980.

Cook, T. D. and Campbell, D. T., *Quasi-Experimentation: Design and Analysis Issues for Field Settings* (Chicago: Rand McNally College Publishing Company, 1979).

Couger, J. D. and Zawacki, R. A., "What Motivates D P Professionals," *Datamation*, September, 1978, pp. 116-23.

Data Communications, "On-line Homework a Prelude to New Job Status?" October 1980, pp. 31-36.

Davis, G. B., *Management Information Systems: Conceptual Foundations, Structure, and Development* (New York: McGraw-Hill, 1974).

Diabold Report, "Office Work in the Home: Scenarios and Prospects for the '80s," Fall 1981.

Dickson, G. W. and Powers, R. F., "MIS Project Management: Myths Opinions and Reality," MISRC Working Paper, WP-71-01, University of Minnesota, 1971.

Dickson, G. W., Senn, J. A., and Chervany, N. L., "Research in Management Information-Decision Systems: The Minnesota Experiments," MISRC Working Paper, WP-75-08, University of Minnesota, 1975.

Dickson, G. W. and Simmons, J. K., "The Behavioral Side of MIS," *Business Horizons* 13, no. 4, August 1970, pp. 59-71.

Dixon, W. J. and Brown, M. B. (eds.), *BMDP-79: Biomedical Computer Programs, P-Series* (Berkeley: University of California Press, 1979).

Downing-Faircloth, M., "Would Working at Home Be Wise?" *Personal Computing*, May 1982, pp. 42-46.

Dubiel, F. A., "Management Opinion," *Administrative Management*, p. 104.

Dunnette, M. D., "Performance Equals Ability and What?," The Center for the Study of Organizational Performance and Human Effectiveness.

EDP Analyzer, "Can Telecommunications Replace Travel?" 20, no. 4, April 1982.

Ewing, T., "Vermont Software House: A Home for 'Rural Technologists,'" *Software*, January 21, 1980.

Flanagan, J. C., "The Critical Incident Technique," *Psychological Bulletin*, 51, no. 4, July 1954.

Ford, R. N., *Motivation Through the Work Itself*, American Management Association, Inc., 1969.

Freiberger, P., "Telecommuting Makes Inroads," *Infoworld*, October 12, 1981, pp. 12-13.

Galbraith, J. R., "Organizational Design: An Information Processing View," *TIMS Interfaces* 4, no. 3, May 1974, pp. 28-36.

Gibson, C. F., "A Methodology for Implementation Research," in *Implementing Operations Research/Management Science*, ed. by R. L. Schultz and D. P. Slevin (New York: American Elsevier Publishing Co., Inc., 1975), pp. 53-73.

[Grangeis, M.], "The Potential for Telecommuting," *Business Week*, January 26, 1981, pp. 94-103.

Guetzkow, H., "Communications in Organizations," in *Handbook of Organizations*, ed. by J. G. March (Chicago: Rand McNally & Co., 1965), pp. 534-73.

Havelock, R. and Havelock, M., "Our Contempory Knowledge of the Change Process," *Training for Change Agents* (University of Michigan: Institute for Social Research, 1973).

Hackman, J. R. and Lawler, E. E., "Employee Reactions to Job Characteristics," *Journal of Applied Psychology*, 1971, pp. 259-86.

Hackman, J. R. and Oldham, G. R., "A New Strategy for Job Enrichment," Technical Report No. 3, Department of Administrative Sciences, Yale University, 1974.

———, "Motivation Through the Design of Work: Test of a Theory," Technical Report No. 6, Department of Administrative Sciences, Yale University, 1974.

Hackman, J. R. et al., "A New Strategy for Job Enrichment," *California Management Review* 17, no. 4, 1975.

Handy, C., "The Changing Shape of Work," *Organizational Dynamics*, Autumn 1980.

Hannagan, T. A., "A Banking Case Study," *Auerbach* 005.0001.006.

Harkness, R. C., *Technology Assessment of Telecommunications/Transportation Interactions* (Menlo Park, California: Stanford Research Institute, 1977).

Heller, D. K., "More Corporations Endorse Telecommuting for Data Processors," *Infoworld*, December 14, 1981, p. 18.

Herzberg, F., *Work and the Nature of Man* (Cleveland: World Publishing, 1966).

Irving, C., "Beating the Computer Rush with Home Computers," *San Francisco Examiner*, April 8, 1981, p. 1.

Ives, B., "Enriching the Person-Machine Interface: An Investigation of the Relationship between Task Variables and Outcome for Alternative Data Entry Settings and Technologies," Ph.D. dissertation, University of Minnesota, 1980.

Johansen, R., Vallee, J., and Spangler, K., *Electronic Meetings: Technical Alternatives and Social Choices* (Reading, Mass.: Addison-Wesley Publishing Co., 1979).

Johnson, J., "Managers Plug into Computers," *Minneapolis Star*, May 14, 1980, p. 1B.

Katz, D. and Kahn, R. L., *The Social Psychology of Organizations,* 2nd edition (New York: John Wiley & Sons, 1978).

Keen, P., "Information Systems and Organizational Change," *Communication of the ACM* 24 no. 1, January 1981, p. 25.

Kiron, A., "You'll Never Have to Go to Work Again," *Washington Post*, August 24, 1969, p. B5.

Kling, R., "Social Analysis of Computing: Theoretical Perspectives in Recent Empirical Research," *Computer Surveys* 12, no. 1, March 1980.

Kolb, O. and Frohman, A., "An Organizational Development Approach to Consulting," *Sloan Management Review* 12, Fall 1970, pp. 51-56

Kraemer, K. L., "Telecommunications-Transportation Substitution and Energy Productivity: A Re-Examination," University of California, Irvine: Public Policy Research Organization, June 1981.

Kuhn, T. S., *The Structure of Scientific Revolutions* (Chicago: The University of Chicago Press, 1970).

Lawler, E. E., *Motivation in Work Organizations* (Monterey: Brooks/Cole Publishing Co., 1973).

Leavitt, H. J., "Applied Organizational Change in Industry: Structural, Technological and Humanistic Approaches," in: J. C. March (ed.), *Handbook of Organizations* (Chicago: Rand McNally, 1965).

Lederberg, J., "Digital Communications and the Conduct of Science: The New Literacy," *Proceedings of the IEEE* 66, no. 11, November 1979, pp. 1314-19.

Leduc, N. F., "Communicating Through Computers," *Telecommunications Policy*, September 1979, pp. 237-52.

Locke, E. F., "Motivational Effects of Knowledge and Results: Knowledge or Goal Setting?" *Journal of Applied Psychology* 51, 1967, pp. 324-29.

Lucas, H. C., *Why Information Systems Fail* (New York: Columbia University Press, 1975).

———, "Empirical Evidence for a Descriptive Model of Implementation," *MIS Quarterly*, June 1978, pp. 27-42.

Macrae, N., "How to Survive in the Age of Telecommuting," *Management Review*, November 1978.

Manning, R. A. et al., "Alternative Work Site Programs," Control Data Corporation report presented to the Office Technology Research Group, October 1981.

Martin, J., *Telematic Society — A Challenge for Tomorrow* (New Jersey: Prentice-Hall, Inc., 1981).

Mason, R. O., "Forming the Social Contract for the Information Society," *Proceedings of the First International Conference on Information Systems,* Philadelphia, December 1980, pp. 69-74.

Melcher, A. J., *Structure and Process of Organizations: A Systems Approach* (New Jersey: Prentice-Hall, Inc., 1976).

Miller, J. G., *Living Systems* (New York: McGraw-Hill, 1978).

Mini-Micro Systems, "Analyzing Commodity Futures with a Micro," *Mini-Micro Systems*, January 1979, pp. 81-83.

Mumford, E. et al., "A Participative Approach to the Design of Computer Systems," *Impact of Science on Society* 28, no. 3, 1978, pp. 235-53.

Nadler, D. A. and Tushman, M. L., "A Model for Diagnosing Organizational Behavior," *Organizational Dynamics*, Autumn 1980.

Nicholson, T. et al., "Commuting by Computer," *Newsweek*, May 4, 1981, pp. 58-61.

Nie, N. H. et al., *SCSS: A User's Guide to the SCSS Conversational System* (New York: McGraw-Hill Book Company, 1980).

Nilles, J. M. et al., *The Telecommunication Transportation Tradeoff* (New York: John Wiley & Sons, 1977).

Olson, M., "An Investigation of Organizational Contingencies Associated with Structure of the Information Services Function," Ph.D. dissertation, University of Minnesota, 1978.

———, "Remote Office Work: Changing Work Patterns in Space and Time," *Communications of the ACM* 26, no. 3, March 1983, pp. 182-87.

Patner, M. M., "Careers: Life Inside an Electronic Cottage," *Washington Post*, December 30, 1981.

Paul, L., "First Large-Scale Computer, ENIAC, Turns 35 Years Old," *Computerworld*, March 2, 1981, p. 1.

Peele E., "How to Make Telecommuting Work," *Personal Computing*, May 1982, p. 38.

Perry, G. M., "Developing a Cost Justified Nation-Wide Communications Network: A Systematic Approach," *MIS Quarterly* 5, no. 3, September 1980, pp. 17-29.

Pollack, A., "Rising Trend of Computer Age: Employees Who Work at Home,"*New York Times*, March 12, 1981, p. 1.

Porat, M. U., *The Information Economy: Definition and Measurement* (Washington, D. C.: U. S. Department of Commerce, 1977).

"A Preamble to Change," *Personal Computing*, May 1982, p. 5

Roy, D. F., "Work Satisfaction and Social Reward in Quota Achievement: An Analysis of Piecework Incentive," *American Sociological Review* 18, 1953, pp. 507-14.

Schein, E., "The Mechanisms of Change," *The Planning of Change* (New Jersey: Prentice-Hall, 1969), pp. 98-107.

Schmitt, J. W. and Kozar, K. A., "Management's Role in Information System Development Failures: A Case Study," *MIS Quarterly* 2, no. 2, June 1978, pp. 7-16.

Stedry, A. C., and Kay, E., "The Effects of Goal Difficulty on Performance: A Field Experiment," *Behavioral Science* 2, November 1966, pp. 459-70.

Stibbens, S., "People: The Cost of Finding, Hiring and Training," *Infosystems*, January 1981, p. 46.

Tapscott, D. et al., "Towards a Methodology for User-Driven Design of Electronic Office Systems," *Proceedings from Distributed Computing*, September 1980.

Toffler, A., *The Third Wave* (New York: William Morrow & Co., Inc., 1980).

Turoff, M., *Initial Specifications, Electronic Information Exchange System (EIE)*, Computerized Conferencing and Communications Center, New Jersey Institute of Technology, Newark, New Jersey, Research Report No. 1.

———, "The Future of Computer Conferencing," *The Futurist* 9, no. 4, 1976, pp. 182-95.

Turner, A. N. and Lawrence, P. R., *Industrial Jobs and the Worker* (Boston: Harvard Graduate School of Business Administration, 1965).

Uhlig, R. P., "Human Factors in Computer Message Systems," *Datamation*, May 1977, pp. 121-26.

Vallee, J., "Network Conferencing," *Datamation*, May 1974, pp. 85-86.

Vallee, J., Johansen, R., Lupinski, H., and Wilson, T., "Pragmatics and Dynamics of Computer Conferencing: A Summary of Findings From the Forum Project," *Proceedings of the Third International Conference on Computer Communications*, 1976, p. 210

Van Gigch, J. P., *Applied General Systems Theory* (New York: Harper & Row, 1978).

Vicker, R., "Computer Terminals Allow More People to Work at Home Instead of Commuting," *Wall Street Journal*, August 4, 1981, pp. 48-49.

Vroom, V., *Work and Motivation* (New York: John Wiley & Sons, 1969).

Wall, V. D., and Boyd, J. A., "Channel Variation and Attitude Change," *Journal of Communication* 21, 1971, pp. 362-67.

Weiss, D. J., Dawis, R. V., England, G. W., and Lofquist, L. H., *Minnesota Studies in Vocational Rehabilitation: 22, Manual for the Minnesota Satisfaction Questionnaire*. Vocational Psychology Research, University of Minnesota, 1967.

Wexley, K. N. and Yukl, G. A., *Organizational Behavior and Personnel Psychology* (Homewood Ill.: Richard D. Irwin, Inc., 1977).

Zmud, R., "Individual Differences and MIS Success: A Review of the Empirical Literature," *Management Science* 25, October 1979, pp. 966-79.

Index